# Hands-On Enterprise Java Microservices with Eclipse MicroProfile

Build and optimize your microservice architecture with Java

**Cesar Saavedra**
**Heiko W. Rupp**
**Jeff Mesnil**
**Pavol Loffay**
**Antoine Sabot-Durand**
**Scott Stark**

**BIRMINGHAM - MUMBAI**

# Hands-On Enterprise Java Microservices with Eclipse MicroProfile

Copyright © 2019 Packt Publishing

**Commissioning Editor:** Kunal Chaudhari
**Acquisition Editor:** Denim Pinto
**Content Development Editor:** Rohit Kumar Singh
**Senior Editor:** Afshaan Khan
**Technical Editor:** Ketan Kamble
**Copy Editor:** Safis Editing
**Project Coordinator:** Prajakta Naik
**Proofreader:** Safis Editing
**Indexer:** Manju Arasan
**Production Designer:** Alishon Mendonsa

First published: August 2019

Production reference: 1300819

Published by Packt Publishing Ltd.
Livery Place
35 Livery Street
Birmingham
B3 2PB, UK.

ISBN 978-1-83864-310-2

www.packt.com

Packt.com

Subscribe to our online digital library for full access to over 7,000 books and videos, as well as industry leading tools to help you plan your personal development and advance your career. For more information, please visit our website.

## Why subscribe?

- Spend less time learning and more time coding with practical eBooks and Videos from over 4,000 industry professionals

- Improve your learning with Skill Plans built especially for you

- Get a free eBook or video every month

- Fully searchable for easy access to vital information

- Copy and paste, print, and bookmark content

Did you know that Packt offers eBook versions of every book published, with PDF and ePub files available? You can upgrade to the eBook version at www.packt.com and as a print book customer, you are entitled to a discount on the eBook copy. Get in touch with us at customercare@packtpub.com for more details.

At www.packt.com, you can also read a collection of free technical articles, sign up for a range of free newsletters, and receive exclusive discounts and offers on Packt books and eBooks.

# Contributors

## About the authors

**Cesar Saavedra** has been working in the IT industry since 1990 and holds a master of science degree in computer science and an MBA. He has worked as a developer, consultant, technical seller, and technical marketer throughout his career. He currently does technical product marketing for Red Hat JBoss EAP, Eclipse MicroProfile, OpenJDK, Quarkus, and Jakarta EE. He also manages technical marketing for the runtimes, integration, **Business Process Management** (**BPM**), and rules management portfolio, and works closely with engineering and product management on thought leadership. Cesar has authored white papers, e-Books, and blog posts, and is a conference and webinar speaker, giving presentations to customers and partners.

*I would like to thank my wife, Isabelle, and my children, Angeline and Max, for their unwavering support.*

**Heiko W. Rupp** is an open source enthusiast with more than a decade of experience working at Red Hat in the area of middleware monitoring and management. In this role, he has been project lead of the RHQ and Hawkular monitoring systems and has also contributed to various other projects, including Kiali.

Currently, he is helping to define the next route to be taken by Java microservices with his work on Eclipse MicroProfile. As such, he is the specification lead of the Eclipse MicroProfile Metrics effort and is also contributing to other specifications. Heiko has written the first German book about JBoss AS and one of the first German books on EJB3. He lives with his family in Stuttgart, Germany.

*I would like to thank my family, whose support enables me to work on projects like this book.*

**Jeff Mesnil** is employed by Red Hat as a senior software engineer and currently works for JBoss, Red Hat's middleware division, on the WildFly and JBoss EAP application servers. He is a member of the core team in charge of developing the internals of the application servers and heads up its messaging subsystem (which provides the JMS API).

Previously, he contributed to the HornetQ messaging broker that was integrated into WildFly and EAP.

He is a proponent of open source development and all the code he writes, either professionally or privately, is available under open source licenses. Nowadays, it is mostly hosted on GitHub.

He has a keen interest in messaging systems and has written several open source libraries related to messaging.

**Pavol Loffay** is senior software engineer at Red Hat. Pavol is working on observability tools for microservice architectures. He is mostly involved in the tracing domain, where he is an active committer on the Jaeger and OpenTracing projects. He is also a member of the **OpenTracing Specification Council** (**OTSC**) and a lead for the MicroProfile-OpenTracing specification. He has authored many blog posts and given presentations at several conferences. In his free time, Pavol likes to climb mountains and ski steep slopes in the Alps.

**Antoine Sabot-Durand** is a Java champion who works for Red Hat, where he leads the Java EE, now Jakarta EE CDI, spec. He is involved in various projects linked to the CDI ecosystem, MicroProfile, and Jakarta EE. He is also a member of the Devoxx France committee. He lives in France with his wife and three children.

**Scott Stark** began his career in chemical engineering, got steered into parallel computers as part of his PhD work, and then made software his career, beginning with a stint in finance on Wall Street. He then got into open source with the fledgling JBoss company, working on the application server and Java EE. He has worked with microkernel efforts, the IoT, standards, Jakarta EE, Eclipse MicroProfile, and Quarkus. He lives in the Pacific Northwest with his wife.

*I would like to thank my wife, Evening, and furry children, Colette and d'Artagnan.*

# About the reviewers

**David R. Heffelfinger** is an independent consultant based in the Washington D.C. area. He is a Java champion, a member of the NetBeans Dream Team, and is a part of the JavaOne content committee.

He has written several books on Java EE, application servers, NetBeans, and JasperReports. His previous titles include *Java EE 7 Development with NetBeans 8*, *Java EE 7 with GlassFish 4 Application Server*, and *JasperReports 3.5 for Java Developers*, and others. David has been a speaker at conferences such as JavaOne and Oracle Code on multiple occasions.

He has also been a speaker at NetBeans Day in San Francisco and Montreal, showcasing NetBeans features that enhance the development of Java EE applications. You can follow him on Twitter at @ensode.

**Yogesh Prajapati** is an engineer with experience of the architecture, design, and development of scalable and distributed enterprise applications.

He authored the book *Java Hibernate Cookbook*, published by Packt. He has more than 8 years' experience with different aspects of Java, Spring, and cloud development, such as REST and microservices, with hands-on experience in technologies/frameworks including Backbase, Hibernate, AWS Cloud, Google Cloud, Node.js, JavaScript, Angular, MongoDB, and Docker.

He is currently working as a lead full stack consultant at dotin Inc. – The Personality DNA Company.

He completed his Master of Computer Applications from Gujarat University. You can follow Yogesh on his blog – kode12.

# Packt is searching for authors like you

If you're interested in becoming an author for Packt, please visit authors.packtpub.com and apply today. We have worked with thousands of developers and tech professionals, just like you, to help them share their insight with the global tech community. You can make a general application, apply for a specific hot topic that we are recruiting an author for, or submit your own idea.

# Table of Contents

# Section 4: A Working MicroProfile Example

# Section 5: A Peek into the Future

# Preface

This book will help you learn about Eclipse MicroProfile, an open source specification for enterprise Java microservices that started back in 2016, along with its background and history, its value proposition to organizations and businesses, its community governance, the current Eclipse MicroProfile sub-projects (more are being added as the open source project evolves), its implementations, and its interoperability. It will also provide a peek into the future direction of Eclipse MicroProfile, a sample application in Red Hat's implementation of Eclipse MicroProfile in Thorntail, one of the runtimes provided by Red Hat Runtimes, and guidance and considerations for running Eclipse MicroProfile in hybrid-cloud and multi-cloud environments. This book will follow a step-by-step approach to help you understand the Eclipse MicroProfile project and its implementations in the market.

## Who this book is for

This book is for Java developers who wish to create enterprise microservices. To get the most out of this book, you need to be familiar with Java EE and the concept of microservices.

## What this book covers

Chapter 1, *Introduction to Eclipse MicroProfile,* frames the discussion within the context of the digital economy and describes what an enterprise Java microservice is and what the rest of the book will cover.

Chapter 2, *Governance and Contributions,* covers governance, processes, and how to contribute to the MicroProfile project.

Chapter 3, *MicroProfile Config and Fault Tolerance,* goes over config and fault tolerance in MicroProfile sub-projects in detail, explaining what problem each solves and giving code examples for each.

Chapter 4, *MicroProfile Health Check and JWT Propagation,* takes you through the Health Check and JWT Propagation sub-projects, helping you understand what challenges they tackle with the help of code examples.

Chapter 5, *MicroProfile Metrics and OpenTracing*, discusses the Metrics and OpenTracing sub-projects and the problems they solve. You will learn how to work with code examples of these sub-projects.

Chapter 6, *MicroProfile OpenAPI and Type-Safe REST Client*, covers two more sub-projects: OpenAPI and type-safe REST client. This chapter will help you work with code examples and understand the utility of these sub-projects in solving your enterprise problems.

Chapter 7, *MicroProfile Implementations, Quarkus, and Interoperability via the Conference Application*, provides details on the implementations of MicroProfile that are currently available on the market and discusses the project's progress to date. It also delves into *The Conference Application*, a demo that showcases the integration of different vendors' implementations of MicroProfile.

Chapter 8, *A Working Eclipse MicroProfile Code Sample*, provides a fully working project developed using MicroProfile (based on the *Conference Application*) and also gives coordinates to download the assets described.

Chapter 9, *Reactive Programming and Future Developments*, goes over present APIs currently being incubated/developed and APIs being discussed for future inclusion in the MicroProfile specification. In addition, it covers MicroProfile candidate APIs for reactive programming as well as potential future relationships between MicroProfile and Jakarta EE.

Chapter 10, *MicroProfile in Multi-Cloud Environments*, discusses how MicroProfile is a great specification for microservices-based applications in the cloud and provides guidance and considerations for using MicroProfile in hybrid-cloud and multi-cloud environments.

# To get the most out of this book

A basic understanding of microservices and enterprise Java is required. Other installation and setup instructions are provided where necessary.

# Download the example code files

You can download the example code files for this book from your account at www.packt.com. If you purchased this book elsewhere, you can visit www.packtpub.com/support and register to have the files emailed directly to you.

You can download the code files by following these steps:

1. Log in or register at `www.packt.com`.
2. Select the **Support** tab.
3. Click on **Code Downloads**.
4. Enter the name of the book in the **Search** box and follow the onscreen instructions.

Once the file is downloaded, please make sure that you unzip or extract the folder using the latest version of:

- WinRAR/7-Zip for Windows
- Zipeg/iZip/UnRarX for Mac
- 7-Zip/PeaZip for Linux

The code bundle for the book is also hosted on GitHub at `https://github.com/PacktPublishing/Hands-On-Enterprise-Java-Microservices-with-Eclipse-MicroProfile`. In case there's an update to the code, it will be updated on the existing GitHub repository.

We also have other code bundles from our rich catalog of books and videos available at `https://github.com/PacktPublishing/`. Check them out!

# Download the color images

We also provide a PDF file that has color images of the screenshots/diagrams used in this book. You can download it here: `https://static.packt-cdn.com/downloads/9781838643102_ColorImages.pdf`.

# Conventions used

There are a number of text conventions used throughout this book.

`CodeInText`: Indicates code words in text, database table names, folder names, filenames, file extensions, pathnames, dummy URLs, user input, and Twitter handles. Here is an example: "The `checks` array object type consists of a required `name` and `status` string, along with an optional `data` object that contains optional `key` and `value` pairs."

A block of code is set as follows:

```
package org.eclipse.microprofile.health;

@FunctionalInterface
public interface HealthCheck {
  HealthCheckResponse call();
}
```

Any command-line input or output is written as follows:

```
Scotts-iMacPro:jwtprop starksm$ curl http://localhost:8080/jwt/secureHello;
echo
Not authorized
```

**Bold**: Indicates a new term, an important word, or words that you see on screen. For example, words in menus or dialog boxes appear in the text like this. Here is an example: "The advent and accessibility of the internet created a **critical category-formation time** opportunity for organizations."

 Warnings or important notes appear like this.

 Tips and tricks appear like this.

# Get in touch

Feedback from our readers is always welcome.

**General feedback**: If you have questions about any aspect of this book, mention the book title in the subject of your message and email us at customercare@packtpub.com.

**Errata**: Although we have taken every care to ensure the accuracy of our content, mistakes do happen. If you have found a mistake in this book, we would be grateful if you would report this to us. Please visit www.packtpub.com/submit/errata, selecting your book, clicking on the Errata Submission Form link, and entering the details.

**Piracy**: If you come across any illegal copies of our works in any form on the internet, we would be grateful if you would provide us with the location address or website name. Please contact us at copyright@packt.com with a link to the material.

**If you are interested in becoming an author**: If there is a topic that you have expertise in, and you are interested in either writing or contributing to a book, please visit authors.packtpub.com.

# Reviews

Please leave a review. Once you have read and used this book, why not leave a review on the site that you purchased it from? Potential readers can then see and use your unbiased opinion to make purchase decisions, we at Packt can understand what you think about our products, and our authors can see your feedback on their book. Thank you!

For more information about Packt, please visit packt.com.

# Section 1: MicroProfile in the Digital Economy

In this section, you will learn why microservices are important in the digital economy and how MicroProfile addresses the need for enterprise Java microservices. In addition, you will also learn about the sub-projects that currently make up MicroProfile, its value proposition to organizations and developers, and its current processes and governance (that is, how things get done).

This section contains the following chapters:

- Chapter 1, *Introduction to Eclipse MicroProfile*
- Chapter 2, *Governance and Contributions*

# 1
# Introduction to Eclipse MicroProfile

Eclipse MicroProfile is a set of specifications for microservices written in the Java language. It is a project that is community-driven with many implementations in the market. The project, first announced in June 2016, continues to develop a set of common **Application Programming Interfaces** (**APIs**) for implementing Java microservices suitable for modern application development techniques, architectures, and environments. In this chapter, you will learn about the origin and importance of Eclipse MicroProfile.

The following topics will be covered in this chapter:

- Enterprise Java microservices
- Forces that fuel the digital economy and the need for multi-speed IT
- Introducing Eclipse MicroProfile
- MicroProfile value proposition

## Enterprise Java microservices

Application development no longer consists of using a single high-level programming language that runs on your favorite operating system. Nowadays, there are a myriad of languages, specifications, frameworks, proprietary and open source software and tools, underlying deployment infrastructures, and development methodologies that programmers need to learn to develop modern applications. Development at IT organizations has become polyglot, that is, multiple programming languages are used depending on the needs of specific projects. In this age of the cloud, containers, microservices, reactive programming, 12-factor applications, serverless, MINI services, polyglot environments, and so on, developers now have the option to choose the right tool for their task, making them more effective and productive.

With the recent move of Java EE to the Eclipse Foundation under the new name of Jakarta EE, MicroProfile will play a very important role in the future of Enterprise Java because of its synergy with Jakarta EE and the potential ways it can influence it.

The advent of the cloud and mobile, along with the acceleration of open and the **Internet of Things** (**IoT**) have brought about the digital economy. While this has opened up new markets, it has also imposed new demands on businesses and their IT organizations, which are now required to not only support and maintain traditional workloads but also deliver new applications at a faster pace.

Many technologies, languages, architectures, and frameworks have become popular within organizations in an attempt to tackle these new demands. One of these is microservices, specifically, Enterprise Java microservices, since Java is still one of the most popular languages in IT companies. But what is an Enterprise Java microservice?

An Enterprise Java microservice has the following features:

- It is written using the Java language.
- It can use any Java framework.
- It can use any Java API.
- It must be enterprise-grade; that is, reliable, available, scalable, secure, robust, and performant.
- It must fulfill the characteristics of microservice architectures as listed at `https://martinfowler.com/microservices/`, which are as follows:
  - Componentization via services
  - Organized around business capabilities
  - Products not projects
  - Smart endpoints and dumb pipes
  - Decentralized governance
  - Decentralized data management
  - Infrastructure automation
  - Design for failure
  - Evolutionary design

# Forces that fuel the digital economy

The terms **digital economy** and **digital transformation** describe the convergence of four different forces that are changing the needs of businesses: mobile, cloud, IoT, and open source:

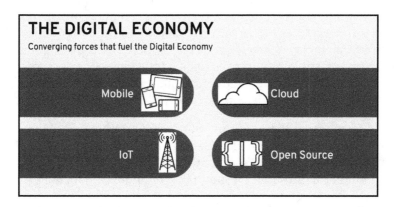

Before the internet, organizations required brick-and-mortar stores or phone lines to conduct their businesses. The advent and accessibility of the internet created a **critical category-formation time** opportunity for organizations. Businesses started to use the internet mainly as a storefront or display in order to drive people to their brick-and-mortar stores. It was also used for advertising purposes.

Soon after this, businesses began adding the ability to purchase things online, and companies, such as Amazon, realized that they could capitalize on the economies-of-scale, product aggregation, consolidation, recommendation, and pricing optimization that an online store could provide. This was the very beginning of cloud and cloud-native applications. This is the first force that fueled the digital economy.

But what really accelerated the digital needs of businesses was the appearance of the second focus mobile devices, which connected even more people to the internet. More people now had a digital presence on the internet and businesses realized that these people were a new market that they could exploit. This new market required applications to scale to what people now call the **internet scale.** But paying for software licenses for this type of scalability was too expensive and prohibitive. This is where open source software, the third force that fueled the digital economy, came to the rescue. The power of the community accelerated the development of open source projects via crowdsourcing and open source collaboration. Anyone from anywhere in the globe could contribute to open source projects. Likewise, internet-scale companies, such as Amazon, Netflix, and Lyft, either use open source software or have created and contributed open source to the community.

Another benefit of open source software is its adoption of subscription-type support (for organizations that require external support for the software they run in production), which is significantly cheaper than software licensing. The growth of open source software fulfilled this need in the market, and companies such as Red Hat, purveyors of open source software, have succeeded in delivering enterprise-grade open source solutions.

As virtualization technologies matured and companies built and proved out internet-scale technologies and infrastructures, they realized that they could rent out these resources, such as compute and memory, to anybody. Consumption-based pricing made these resources even more accessible. Companies realized the value of saving costs, productivity, and speed-to-market of the cloud and started rushing to adopt this new model. Major companies such as Microsoft, Google, and Amazon all have cloud offerings.

IoT is the last and fourth force that is fueling the digital economy. Like the data generated by the digital presence of each person using the internet, IoT also generates large amounts of data that can be exploited to make sound business decisions. IoT demands internet-scale technologies and infrastructures that the cloud and big data technologies fulfill.

The convergence of these four different forces means that organizations have to adapt in the way they create and maintain business applications, thus affecting the speed at which they introduce innovation to their organizations. This is what is known as multi-speed IT, which we will discuss in more detail in the following section.

# Multi-speed IT

Implementing and delivering applications as fast as possible is not a new requirement. In fact, since the invention of the first computer, increasing efficiency has always been in the minds of computer scientists. High-level programming languages, encapsulation, reusability, inheritance, event-driven design, SOA, microservices, machine learning, and AI, are all concepts that address the challenge of doing things faster. With each wave of new technology, the gearbox adds a new speed requirement to the evolution of how we develop and deliver software. The digital economy has added another high-speed gear to the gearbox.

Businesses need to adapt to the new demands of the digital economy. Not only do they have to create, run, and support traditional-style applications, but also applications that conform to the new demands of the digital economy. They have to support both waterfall and DevOps processes, hybrid cloud infrastructures, and SOA and microservice architectures.

This imposes many challenges on IT organizations, whose processes, people, and technology have all been geared toward the implementation, delivery, and maintenance of traditional-style applications. Many organizations have already embarked on, or are starting, their journey of digital transformation, which addresses the challenges of the digital economy. This journey includes changes in technologies, frameworks, languages, and processes for the development, delivery, integration, and maintenance of applications.

Whether you call it bimodal IT (`https://www.gartner.com/it-glossary/bimodal`) or a business technology strategy (`https://go.forrester.com/wp-content/uploads/Forrester-False-Promise-of-Bimodal-IT.pdf`), the fact is that IT needs to deliver faster than ever before on the needs of the business, for both existing and new applications. This means IT needs to also speed up the maintenance and delivery of existing applications while exclusively adopting Agile methodologies for new applications. This does not preclude, however, the need to still use different development processes, release cycles, and support timelines to handle existing applications versus new applications, which is effectively the multi-speed nature of IT.

# Introducing Eclipse MicroProfile

Java EE has been an extremely successful platform. The **Java Community Process (JCP)** has been the steward of over 20 compatible implementations during its nearly 20-year history, resulting in a $4 billion industry. However, the management of Java EE by Oracle (unintentional or not) of Java EE (unintentional or not) stalled innovations, and while other standards have developed, the Java community worldwide and CIOs at all major enterprises desired an open standard for Java within their enterprise.

In its early stages, J2EE grew somewhat quickly from J2EE 1.2 up to J2EE 1.4, as the platform needed to address the immediate requirements of the enterprise. Beginning with Java EE 5 in May 2006, the pace began to slow down as the platform began to mature, and it was 3 years and 6 months between releases. After Java EE 7, which was released on June 12, 2013, there has been a long delay in its development. Java EE 8 was formally launched in September 2014 at JavaOne, where Oracle announced that it would be completed by JavaOne 2016. But then in June 2015, Oracle updated its release date to the first half of 2017. And again, at JavaOne 2016 (September), Oracle revised the Java EE 8 release date to the end of 2017. Java EE 8 was finally released on September 21, 2017, at JavaOne.

The following diagram shows the evolution timeline:

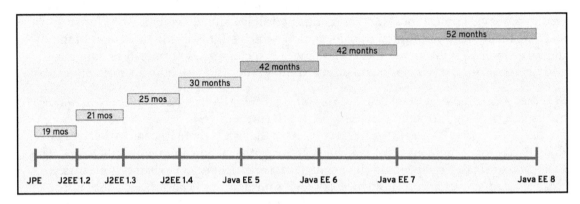

Java EE had been following the slower release cadence that a standards organization typically reflects. A standards-based release cadence by design does not address rapid innovations. And while this was occurring, the digital economy happened, which brought about the popularity and rising use of the cloud, containers, Agile methodologies, DevOps, continuous integration and continuous delivery, microservices, API management, and open source projects (Red Hat has been successful in delivering many of these solutions to the marketplace).

The slowdown in Java EE releases (and maturity) opened the door to competing technologies, such as Spring and Node.js, for example, which were able to fulfill the needs and requirements of digital businesses. In addition to this, many vendors, such as Red Hat and IBM, started innovating with Enterprise Java microservices based on a subset of Java EE and decided to collaborate in the open, potentially providing a wider effort upstream. This culminated in the announcement of Eclipse MicroProfile in June 2016 by many vendors, Java Champions, Java User Groups, and corporations.

Since MicroProfile was announced on June 27, 2016, at DevNation, a lot has happened. MicroProfile v 1.0 was released on September 19, 2016. Its implementation interoperability was demonstrated in November 2016 at Devoxx Belgium, where Red Hat, IBM, Tomitribe, and Payara demonstrated a unified web application (known as the *Conference Application*) with underlying microservices that had been developed separately by each vendor using MicroProfile. Additionally, MicroProfile became part of the Eclipse Foundation as an incubation project on December 14, 2016. New members, including SOUJava, Hazelcast, Fujitsu, Hammock, kumuluzEE, Oracle, Lightbend, and Microsoft, have joined the MicroProfile project. The complete list of members can be found at `https://microprofile.io/`.

Eclipse MicroProfile is a community-driven innovation project whose goal is to work on microservice patterns for Enterprise Java and to integrate applications with the infrastructures they run on (that is, a cloud environment) with patterns such as health checks and metrics. The focus of Eclipse MicroProfile is rapid collaborative innovation and this is why the project has a time-boxed release schedule, with each release including incremental updates or new features, and there is no guarantee of backward compatibility across releases. The Eclipse MicroProfile community is composed of individuals, vendors, and organizations.

Eclipse MicroProfile is not Java EE or a subset of Java EE. This confusion occurred because the first release of MicroProfile (before it became part of the Eclipse Foundation) was a collection of three Java EE APIs, namely, CDI, JSON-P, and JAX-RS. The MicroProfile community purposely made the first release of MicroProfile small because they wanted the community to decide the best path of evolution for the project.

The MicroProfile community took a *no need to reinvent the wheel* approach for the first release and chose three enterprise-grade, market- and production-proven APIs from Java EE to get started. In fact, MicroProfile utilizes some existing Java EE APIs and combines them with new APIs to create a platform for Java microservice architectures.

At the time of writing this book, Eclipse MicroProfile consists of 12 APIs (or sub-projects) under the project umbrella. Four of them come from Java EE APIs: CDI, JSON-P, JAX-RS, and JSON-B, and the remaining eight are MicroProfile-specific project. They are as follows:

- Config
- Fault Tolerance
- JWT Propagation
- Health Check
- Metrics
- Open API
- Open Tracing
- REST Client
- CDI (a specification from Java EE)
- JSON-P (a specification from Java EE)
- JAX-RS (a specification from Java EE)
- JSON-B (a specification from Java EE)

Here is a high-level explanation of the requirement that each of the aforementioned APIs fulfills:

- **MicroProfile Config** addresses the need for changing the environmental parameters as an application or microservice moves across development, unit testing, integration/system testing, preproduction, and production environments, for example. MicroProfile Config makes it possible to set or modify configuration data from outside the application without repackaging it.
- **MicroProfile Fault Tolerance** provides different strategies for when an application or microservice encounters a fault. MicroProfile Fault Tolerance provides specifications for constructs such as retries, circuit breakers, bulkheads, and timeouts, among others.
- **MicroProfile JWT Propagation** handles security propagation across microservices.
- **MicroProfile Health Check** fulfills the need to probe the state of a computing node from another machine, that is, a Kubernetes service controller. This specification examines cloud-infrastructure environments where the node state is tracked by automated processes.
- **MicroProfile Metrics** delivers on the need to monitor the essential parameters of a running service, such as the system, application, business- and vendor-specific metrics in order to ensure its reliable operation.
- **MicroProfile Open API** provides Java interfaces and programming models to natively produce OpenAPI v3 documents for RESTful services that can facilitate the management of microservice APIs.
- **MicroProfile Open Tracing** defines the specification for equipping microservices to be traceable in a highly-distributed environment where messages can traverse different architectural tiers and services.
- **MicroProfile REST Client** provides a type-safe approach to invoke RESTful services over HTTP in a consistent and easy-to-reuse fashion.
- **CDI** (a specification from Java EE) handles all aspects of dependency injection.
- **JSON-P** (a specification from Java EE) covers all aspects related to the processing of JSON objects.
- **JAX-RS** (a specification from Java EE) handles all aspects related to RESTful communication.
- **JSON-B** (a specification from Java EE) covers all aspects related from the object to JSON mapping.

It is worth mentioning that all the APIs (or sub-projects) created by the MicroProfile projects are not created in a vacuum. Although anybody can participate and is welcome in any sub-project, members of each sub-project are subject-matter experts with long and extensive expertise and experience. They apply their knowledge gained from the field, considering best practices, past lessons-learned, and other existing open source specifications and projects, to come up with the best approach for the corresponding MicroProfile sub-project.

Eclipse MicroProfile has been evolving rapidly and their versions have been progressively adding more functionality as follows:

- Eclipse MicroProfile 1.1 included Config, which is a MicroProfile sub-project
- Eclipse MicroProfile 1.2 included updates to Config as well as the new MicroProfile sub-projects: JWT Propagation, Metrics, Fault Tolerance, and Health Check.
- Likewise, Eclipse MicroProfile 1.3 included additional brand new MicroProfile sub-projects: Open API, Open Tracing, and Rest Client.
- MicroProfile 1.4 included updates to Config, JWT Propagation, Fault Tolerance, Open Tracing, and Rest Client.
- In addition, MicroProfile 2.0 included the latest updates to CDI, JSON-P, JAX-RS, and the addition of JSON-B, all from Java EE 8. With these releases, Eclipse MicroProfile will offer the same level of functionality to be usable with either Java EE 7 or Java EE 8.
- Eclipse MicroProfile 2.1 included updates to Open Tracing.
- Eclipse MicroProfile 2.2 included updates to Fault Tolerance, Type Safe Rest Client, Open API, and Open Tracing.
- Lastly, MicroProfile 3.0 included updates to Rest Client, and non-backward-compatible changes to Metrics and Health Check.

There are currently many implementations of Eclipse MicroProfile on the market. Eclipse MicroProfile is one of the tools that developers can leverage to solve problems and implement solutions with the enterprise capabilities needed to run workloads in production. In addition, developers familiar with Enterprise Java frameworks, such as Java EE, will find in MicroProfile a natural progression of Enterprise Java into the world of cloud-native application development.

# MicroProfile value proposition

For customers who trust Enterprise Java to run their production workloads, Eclipse MicroProfile provides customers with a vendor-neutral specification for Enterprise Java microservices. Eclipse MicroProfile enables them to better fulfill the needs of the business via improved agility and scalability, faster time-to-market, higher development productivity, easier debugging and maintenance, and continuous integration and continuous deployment.

The benefits customers get by using Eclipse MicroProfile are the same benefits gained by using microservices. In general, according to Martin Fowler, a respected software developer, author, and speaker, microservices provide the following benefits (`https://martinfowler.com/articles/microservice-trade-offs.html`):

- **Strong module boundaries**: Microservices reinforce modular structure, which is particularly important for larger teams.
- **Independent deployment**: Simple services are easier to deploy and, since they are autonomous, they are less likely to cause system failures when things go wrong.
- **Technology diversity**: With microservices, you can mix multiple languages, development frameworks, and data storage technologies.

In addition to the general benefits of microservices, Eclipse MicroProfile specifically provides the following:

- **The benefits of community collaboration**: Eclipse MicroProfile is an open source project run by the community. No single vendor controls or determines the evolution and maturation of the specification.
- **Freedom of choice of implementation**: Many vendors have implemented Eclipse MicroProfile as part of their software stacks and customers have the option to select whichever implementation is the most appropriate for their environment.
- **Faster evolution**: Since Eclipse MicroProfile is an innovation project, new and improved functionality is delivered frequently in time-boxed releases. This allows developers and customers to have these at their fingertips and start leveraging updates in their projects sooner rather than later.
- **Based on decades of experience:** Not only do the specification's subject-matter experts bring with them a vast wealth of experience, expertise, and knowledge, but Eclipse MicroProfile also leverages market-tested and production-proven capabilities in the Java EE APIs that it builds upon, offering maturity to developers.

- **Familiarity with Enterprise Java**: Eclipse MicroProfile builds upon familiar Enterprise Java constructs, making it easy for Enterprise Java developers to adopt.
- **No retraining needed**: Your existing Enterprise Java developers will find Eclipse MicroProfile to be a natural progression of their expertise. There is little to no learning curve. They will be able to leverage their skills.
- **Interoperability:** The different MicroProfile implementations are interoperable, with each one providing users with the freedom to select one, or combine many, MicroProfile implementations in an application.
- **Multiple ways to use the APIs**: Eclipse MicroProfile APIs provide easy-to-use interfaces, such as CDI-based, programmatic, command-line, and file-based (configuration-based) interfaces.
- **A thorough set of artifacts**: Each API includes a **Test Compatibility Kit** (**TCK**), Javadoc, PDF document for download, API Maven artifact coordinates, Git tags, and downloads (specification and source code).
- Many other benefits that are particular to each API. These are discussed in each Eclipse MicroProfile sub-project section throughout this book.

# Summary

In this chapter, we have discussed the new trends in software development, consisting of polyglot deployments using new approaches, such as microservices, containers, mobile, and Internet-of-Things (IoT) running on-premises and in the cloud; and in hybrid or multi-cloud environments. These trends required the evolution of Enterprise Java in the microservices world, which is what MicroProfile addresses. The four forces that fuel the digital economy, namely, cloud, mobile, IoT, and open source, have contributed to the need for organizations to have multi-speed IT departments, which are necessary to maintain and evolve their existing applications as well as to take advantage of new technological trends to develop new applications that can help them to remain competitive.

Eclipse MicroProfile, a vendor-neutral specification founded by the community for the community, is one of these new trends for Enterprise Java microservices. Lastly, Eclipse MicroProfile brings rapid innovation to Enterprise Java by its development agility based on lessons learned and decades of experience by the subject-matter experts who participate in its sub-teams. This chapter has helped you to understand what an Enterprise Java microservice is and what the rest of the book will cover.

In the next chapter, we will go over the governance, that is, the lightweight process that anybody in the community can follow to contribute to the Eclipse MicroProfile project. Additionally, we will examine the contributions made to the project, namely, the Eclipse MicroProfile Starter, which is a sample source code generator contribution.

# Questions

1. What is an Enterprise Java microservice?
2. What are the four forces that fuel the digital economy?
3. Why are IT organizations having to develop and maintain applications at different speeds? What is multi-speed IT?
4. Why are Java and Java EE still important to organizations?
5. What was one of the key reasons that caused MicroProfile to come into existence?
6. What are the APIs/specifications that are part of the MicroProfile umbrella/platform release?
7. What release of MicroProfile introduced the first revolutionary changes?
8. Why is MicroProfile valuable to organizations?

# Governance and Contributions

2

Eclipse MicroProfile is governed by community members. In other words, it is not governed by a single vendor. In addition, it receives contributions from developers and subject-matter experts across a spectrum of organizations, corporations, and individual contributors. The project is characterized by its innovation, speed, and agility via light processes and governance. The topics in this chapter will help you to understand the governance of the MicroProfile project, and you will discover how you can contribute to the MicroProfile project too.

The following topics will be covered in this chapter:

- How the Eclipse MicroProfile project is governed
- How the community collaborates and contributes to its constant innovation
- The Eclipse MicroProfile Starter project—an example source code generator

## Current Eclipse MicroProfile governance

Eclipse MicroProfile is transparent in its operations and decision-making processes, which are intended to be very lightweight. Governance focuses on creating, innovating, and evolving specifications in a collaborative manner.

Eclipse MicroProfile, first and foremost, is an Eclipse project and it, therefore, follows Eclipse processes. This includes committer approvals, project releases, intellectual property safeguarding, license review processes, and more. However, the Eclipse Foundation is flexible enough for projects such as MicroProfile to offer some additional lightweight processes for multiple specifications to move forward in parallel with ways to communicate across and align specifications.

One of these lightweight processes is the Eclipse MicroProfile bi-weekly Hangout meeting/call (whose meeting URL is `https://eclipse.zoom.us/j/949859967`, and whose recordings can be found on the Eclipse MicroProfile YouTube channel at `https://www.youtube.com/channel/UC_Uqc8MYFDoCItFIGheMD_w`), which is open to anybody in the community and serves as a forum where topics brought up by attendees are discussed and decisions are made, from sub-project statuses and release contents to release dates and sub-project creation approvals. It should be noted that MicroProfile is not a standards organization, although it can seem that way. MicroProfile was created by the community for the community, and it moves at the speed that the community determines as it innovates in its different sub-projects. MicroProfile defines specifications that encourage multiple implementations, much like a standards organization. However, MicroProfile truly operates as a fast-evolving open source project whose source code is specifications.

The main means of community communication, discussion, and debate is the Eclipse MicroProfile Google Group (`https://groups.google.com/forum/#!forum/microprofile`). You can use your favorite web browser to read, post, answer, or start forum messages for any MicroProfile-related topic in the Google Group. You can also use the Group's email to start new forum messages. Anybody can start new forum threads to discuss topics, such as potential new functionality to be added to MicroProfile. After the community discusses a new idea at length in the forum and/or the MicroProfile Hangout call, and it's been determined that it is worth furthering the debate, the community decides to create a working group for this new idea, and a lead or a group of leads, who are usually subject-matter experts in the topic at hand, are designated to serve as its facilitators.

One important aspect to note is that the lead or leads of a working group (or sub-project for that matter) do not single-handedly shape or determine the evolution of a specification or what capabilities are included or not. They do not have the power of veto or a final say in the decisions made with respect to their specification. By their sharing of ideas, expertise, past experiences, analysis of existing technologies, and best practices, the working group will come up with their best proposal possible. In addition, all unresolved issues need to be discussed by the community and brought up in the bi-weekly Hangout meeting/call for further debate, if needed. Through discussion, collaboration, and feedback from the community, many points of view are analyzed, allowing the best option or options to bubble up to the top. The working group will establish a recurring weekly or bi-weekly meeting, which is entered in the MicroProfile Google Calendar (`https://calendar.google.com/calendar/embed?src=gbnbc373ga40n0tvbl88nkc3r4%40group.calendar.google.com`). This contains information of all MicroProfile Hangout calls, MicroProfile sub-project calls, and MicroProfile release dates.

While anybody can attend these meetings, there's usually a core number of people that serve as the subject-matter experts who participate in these calls. After a few meetings, the working group decides whether or not the new functionality should be brought up to the MicroProfile Hangout call to discuss its proposal to become a MicroProfile sub-project.

At the MicroProfile Hangout call, a sub-project proposal may be rejected or accepted. It should be said that by the time the sub-project proposal is brought to the MicroProfile Hangout call, most of the discussion of whether or not it should move forward will have taken place already, so the decision taken at the call should really be of no surprise to the sub-project working group. The rejection of a sub-project does not mean that it does not fulfill a specific developmental need, but rather an affirmation that its goals are not a good match to advance the MicroProfile specification, whose goal is the optimization of Enterprise Java for a microservices architecture.

For example, if a sub-project proposal addresses a need that is unrelated to microservices, then the chances are that the sub-project proposal will not move forward as a MicroProfile sub-project. The acceptance of a sub-project means that it effectively addresses a need that enriches the specification toward its goal of optimizing Enterprise Java for a microservices architecture. It is at this moment that a sub-project becomes an official MicroProfile API. Once the sub-project becomes a MicroProfile API, then a determination is made as to whether it should be a standalone sub-project outside the umbrella or a sub-project included in the umbrella MicroProfile releases. A high-level flowchart of this process is as follows:

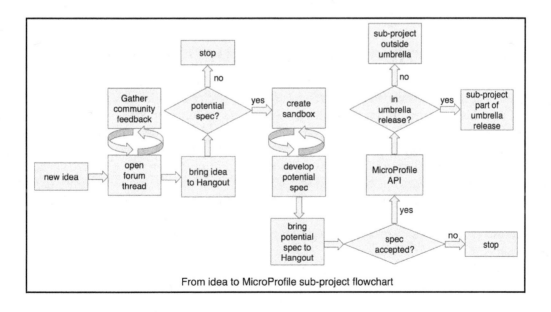

From idea to MicroProfile sub-project flowchart

At the time of writing this book, these are the Eclipse MicroProfile APIs/sub-projects (with the project leads listed):

| MicroProfile API/Sub-project name | Sub-project lead(s) |
|---|---|
| MicroProfile Project Leads | John Clingan and Kevin Sutter |
| Config | Emily Jiang and Mark Struberg |
| Fault Tolerance | Emily Jiang |
| Health Check | Antoine Sabot-Durand |
| JWT Propagation | Scott Stark |
| Metrics | Heiko Rupp |
| OpenAPI | Arthur De Magalhaes |
| OpenTracing | Pavol Loffay |
| Rest Client | John D. Ament and Andy McCright |

Eclipse MicroProfile follows a time-boxed rapid incremental release schedule, which is public and is listed at the Eclipse Foundation MicroProfile Project page (`https://projects.eclipse.org/projects/technology.microprofile`). Major Eclipse MicroProfile releases, for example, from 1.x to 2.x, include major updates to MicroProfile APIs that may introduce breaking changes. Minor releases, that is point releases, include small API updates or new APIs that make the predetermined release date. Currently, the MicroProfile community release windows are in February, June, and November of every year for minor and/or major releases.

# Sandbox approach to open contribution

The creation of a working group for a potential MicroProfile sub-project may also be assigned a sandbox, which is another resource that the MicroProfile community offers to try out new ideas. The sandbox repository, which is a GitHub repository located at `https://github.com/eclipse/microprofile-sandbox`, is for incubating ideas and code examples that will eventually turn into a separate repository for a new specification. Anybody can open pull requests and use the sandbox for experimentation of new ideas and to share code and documentation, which can be used as part of the discussion in the community Google Group, the MicroProfile Hangout calls, or working group meetings. Keeping your pull requests open will also allow discussion of your code and documentation within the community. Potential sub-projects live under the sandbox directory named **proposals** (`https://github.com/eclipse/microprofile-sandbox/tree/master/proposals`).

If you need to accept and merge a pull request, you need to contact one of the MicroProfile project committers (`https://projects.eclipse.org/projects/technology.microprofile/who`) for guidance.

Likewise, if you feel that your idea has reached a level of maturity that deserves its own separate repository, that is graduating out of the sandbox, then you need to contact one of the MicroProfile project committers for guidance and/or reach them via the MicroProfile mailing list: `microprofile@googlegroups.com`. These graduation requests are also discussed at the MicroProfile Hangout call/meeting.

# Umbrella releases versus projects outside the umbrella

Eclipse MicroProfile is composed of a set of specifications, each with a specific focus. For example, the Eclipse MicroProfile Config specification encompasses everything related to configuring parameters for microservices. A version of a specification can be included as part of an umbrella release of Eclipse MicroProfile or be released outside the umbrella. As a concrete example, the latest umbrella release of Eclipse MicroProfile 2.2, which came out on February 12, 2019, included the following specifications:

- Eclipse MicroProfile Open Tracing 1.3
- Eclipse MicroProfile Open API 1.1
- Eclipse MicroProfile Rest Client 1.2
- Eclipse MicroProfile Fault Tolerance 2.0
- Eclipse MicroProfile Config 1.3
- Eclipse MicroProfile Metrics 1.1
- Eclipse MicroProfile JWT Propagation 1.1
- Eclipse MicroProfile Health Check 1.0
- CDI 2.0
- JSON-P 1.1
- JAX-RS 2.1
- JSON-B 1.0

Eclipse MicroProfile, however, also has other specifications that have been released outside the umbrella release. For example, Eclipse MicroProfile Reactive Streams Operators 1.0, which we will cover in Chapter 9, *Reactive Programming and Future Developments*, is a specification that was recently released outside the umbrella. So, why does MicroProfile allow specifications outside the umbrella? Well, the reason is that by releasing outside the umbrella first, it gives the community and end users an opportunity to utilize and test the new technology and, therefore, proving it in real applications before it can be considered for inclusion in the umbrella.

# MicroProfile Starter

MicroProfile Starter is a sample source code generator, whose goal is to aid developers to quickly get started using and exploiting the capabilities of the community-driven open source specification for Enterprise Java microservices, Eclipse MicroProfile, by generating working sample code in a Maven project.

The idea of having MicroProfile Starter has been around since the creation of the project back in mid-2016 and was publicly discussed at Devoxx BE 2016 (the week of November 7, 2016). In its first two weeks of being available, developers around the world have created over 1,200 projects through the MicroProfile Starter project, which is a good and positive indication of its adoption worldwide.

## A quick tour of MicroProfile Starter

Let's take a quick tour of MicroProfile Starter:

1. When you go to the **MicroProfile Starter "Beta"** page, https://start. microprofile.io/, you will see the following landing page:

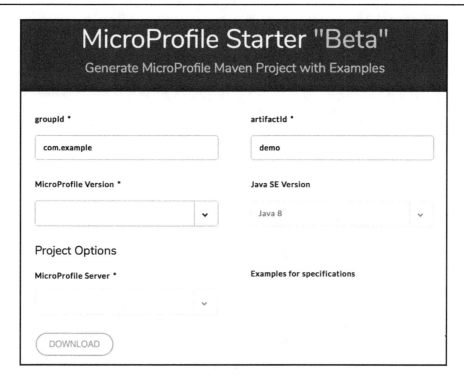

You can accept the defaults for the Maven-related parameters (`https://maven.apache.org/guides/mini/guide-naming-conventions.html`), **groupId** and **artifactId**, or change them to your liking. The **groupId** parameter uniquely identifies your project across all projects, and **artifactId** is the name of the JAR file without the MicroProfile version number. For this tour, accept all of the defaults.

2. Next, select **MicroProfile Version** from the drop-down list:

For this tour, select MicroProfile version **MP 2.1**. Notice that, depending on the version of MicroProfile you select, the number of specifications listed in the **Example for specifications** section will vary. This number depends on how many APIs were included as part of each MicroProfile umbrella release. To find out what APIs were included in each release, please refer to the MicroProfile community presentation (`https://docs.google.com/presentation/d/1BYfVqnBIffh-QDIrPyromwc9YSwIbsawGUECSsrSQB0/edit#slide=id.g4ef35057a0_6_205`).

3. Then, select **MicroProfile Server** from the drop-down list:

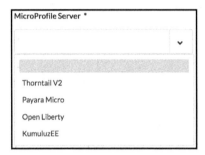

For this tour, select **Thorntail V2**, which is the open source project that Red Hat uses to implement the Eclipse MicroProfile specification.

4. Leave all the **Examples for specifications** checkboxes selected (that is, do not uncheck any of the checkboxes):

This will generate example working code for all of the APIs included in MicroProfile version 2.1.

5. The last step in the samples source code generation process using MicroProfile Starter is to click on the **DOWNLOAD** button, which will create a ZIP archive. Ensure you save the `demo.zip` file to your local drive. Then, unzip `demo.zip` in your local drive. The contents should look like this:

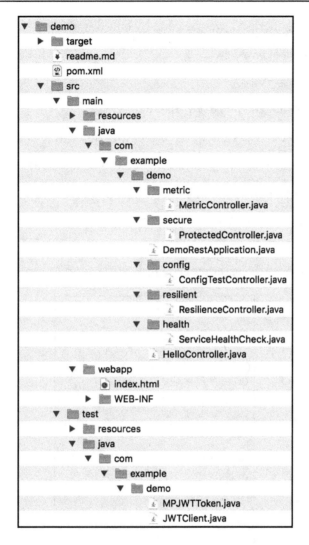

Notice that there's a `readme.md` file in the generated content. This file contains instructions on how to compile and run the generated code, which includes a sample web application that exercises the different capabilities of Eclipse MicroProfile.

6. Change directory to wherever you unzipped the demo project. In my case, I had it in my `Downloads` directory:

```
$ cd Downloads/demo
```

7. Compile the generated sample code by entering the following command:

   ```
   $ mvn clean package
   ```

8. Run the microservice:

   ```
   $ java -jar target/demo-thorntail.jar
   ```

9. After a few seconds, you will see the following message:

   ```
   $ INFO  [org.wildfly.swarm] (main) WFSWARM99999: Thorntail is Ready
   ```

   This indicates that the microservice is up and running.

10. Open your favorite web browser and point it to
    `http://localhost:8080/index.html`.

    This will open up the sample web application, as follows:

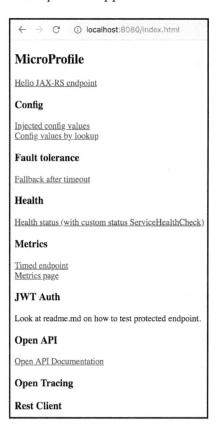

11. To see the capabilities of **MicroProfile Config**, click on **Injected config values**. A window tab will open with the following display:

12. Likewise, if you click on **Config values by lookup**, another window tab will be displayed as follows:

The parameter value's *injected value* and *lookup value* that we saw previously are defined in the ./demo/src/main/resources/META-INF/microprofile-config.properties file, as shown here:

```
$ cat ./src/main/resources/META-INF/microprofile-
config.properties
injected.value=Injected value
value=lookup value
```

13. Imagine that you need to use a different value for the value parameter between development and system testing. You could do this by passing a parameter in the command line when starting the microservice as follows (ensure to exit the running application by pressing *Ctrl + C* on the Terminal window first):

```
$ java -jar target/demo-thorntail.jar -Dvalue=hola
```

14. Now, when you click on **Config values by lookup**, another window tab is displayed:

Note that the source code executing this logic is located in the generated ./src/main/java/com/example/demo/config/ConfigTestControlle r.java file.

15. To see the capabilities of MicroProfile Fault Tolerance, click on **Fallback after timeout**. A window tab will open with the following display:

 For more information on the MicroProfile Config API, please refer to its documentation (https://github.com/eclipse/microprofile-config/releases/download/1.3/microprofile-config-spec-1.3.pdf).

The sample code is exercising the @Fallback annotation in combination with @Timeout. Here's the sample code:

```
@Fallback(fallbackMethod = "fallback") // fallback handler
  @Timeout(500)
  @GET
  public String checkTimeout() {
    try {
      Thread.sleep(700L);
    } catch (InterruptedException e) {
      //
    }
    return "Never from normal processing";
  }
  public String fallback() {
  return "Fallback answer due to timeout";
  }
```

The @Timeout annotation specifies that if the method takes longer than 500 milliseconds to execute, a timeout exception should be thrown. This annotation can be used together with @Fallback, which, in this case, invokes the fallback handler called fallback when the timeout exception occurs. In the previously generated sample code, the timeout exception will always happen because the method is executing—that is, sleeping for 700 milliseconds, which is longer than 500 milliseconds.

Note that the source code executing this logic is located in the generated ./src/main/java/com/example/demo/resilient/ResilienceController.java file.

For more information on the MicroProfile Fault Tolerance API, please refer to its documentation (`https://github.com/eclipse/microprofile-opentracing/releases/download/1.2/microprofile-opentracing-spec-1.2.pdf`).

The MicroProfile community welcomes your feedback as well as collaboration or contributions toward the continued development of the MicroProfile Starter project. To give feedback, you need to click on the **Give Feedback** button in the top-right of the **MicroProfile Starter "Beta"**(`https://start.microprofile.io/`) landing page and create an issue.

The MicroProfile Starter project groups and prioritizes requested items and fixes in milestones with the goal of releasing continuously. The MicroProfile Starter working group meets on a regular basis and if you'd like to help the project with your development skills, please send an email to `microprofile@googlegroups.com` or join the discussion on its Gitter channel (`https://gitter.im/eclipse/microprofile-starter`). The project information, including the location of its source code, can be found at `https://wiki.eclipse.org/MicroProfile/StarterPage`.

# Summary

In this chapter, we learned about the lightweight governance processes of the Eclipse MicroProfile project, its rapid approach to innovation, and how sandboxes are used to foster collaboration and encourage code development and documentation. We also learned about its sub-projects, the leaders of these sub-projects, and how they can be released either standalone or as part of an Eclipse MicroProfile umbrella release.

In addition, you learned about MicroProfile Starter, which is a Maven project generation tool that provides code samples so that developers can get their MicroProfile applications started quickly. Finally, we got a sneak-peek at how an application's properties can be easily modified using Eclipse MicroProfile Config constructs, and how to use the `@Timeout` and `@Fallback` annotations from the Eclipse MicroProfile Fault Tolerance specification.

In the next chapter, we will delve deeper into the Eclipse MicroProfile Config and Eclipse MicroProfile Fault Tolerance specifications and provide code samples on how to use them.

# Questions

1. What are the main means of communication for the MicroProfile community?
2. What is the goal of the bi-weekly MicroProfile Hangout call?
3. What is the role of a sub-project (MicroProfile specification) lead/leads?
4. What is the process followed by a new MicroProfile specification proposal?
5. What is the release schedule that the MicroProfile project follows?
6. What is the goal of the MicroProfile sandbox?
7. What is the difference between projects released under the umbrella/platform MicroProfile release and outside it?
8. What is MicroProfile Starter and what benefits does it provide?

# Section 2: MicroProfile's Current Capabilities

This section goes over the capabilities of the project and its sub-projects, along with code examples.

This section contains the following chapters:

- Chapter 3, *MicroProfile Config and Fault Tolerance*
- Chapter 4, *MicroProfile Health Check and JWT Propagation*
- Chapter 5, *MicroProfile Metrics and OpenTracing*
- Chapter 6, *MicroProfile OpenAPI and the Type-Safe REST Client*

# 3
# MicroProfile Config and Fault Tolerance

In this chapter, we will start by introducing MicroProfile Config as it is the basis for the configuration of other MicroProfile features, in addition to application-level configuration. The MicroProfile Config specification provides a common way to retrieve configuration coming from a variety of sources (properties files, system properties, environment variables, databases, and so on).

The topics we will cover include the following:

- Reading configuration from your application
- Providing additional sources of configuration to your application
- Providing conversion from plain configuration into application-specific objects

## Understanding Eclipse MicroProfile Config

Every application needs some external configuration to adapt its behavior to the runtime platform it's running on. It can range from the HTTP endpoints that the application must connect to, or the size of some internal structures.

These configuration parameters can also come from different sources:

- From the operating system or the container in a cloud-native environment (through the use of environment variables)
- From the Java virtual machine (with system properties)
- From some external configuration files (such as the Java properties file)
- From other places (an LDAP server, database, key-value store, and so on)

On the one hand, these configuration parameters come from many different sources. On the other hand, we want to consume them in the Java application in a simple way that does not depend on the source of the configuration. The Eclipse MicroProfile Config specification addresses this problem.

The MicroProfile Config API is split into two parts that tackle the two sides of the problem:

- The API defines the `Config` and `@ConfigProperty` types that are used by the Java application to get the values of the configuration parameters.
- The API also defines a **Service Provider Interface** (**SPI**) to let other projects (or the Java application itself) provide the sources of configuration parameters.

Implementations of MicroProfile Config must provide default `ConfigSource` implementations that are always available to the application.

For most use cases, the application will mainly be interested in reading configuration from the Config API, which we will cover in the next section.

# Reading configuration from the MicroProfile Config API

The MicroProfile Config specification defines two objects to read the value of configuration parameters:

- The `Config` object to programmatically access the configuration values
- The `@ConfigProperty` annotation to inject the configuration values using **Contexts and Dependency Injection** (**CDI**)

Let's discuss them in detail.

# The Config object

The `org.eclipse.microprofile.config.Config` interface is the entry point to retrieve configuration in a Java application.

There are two ways to get an instance of `Config`:

1. The first (and preferred) way is to use CDI to inject it into the code:

   ```
   @Inject
   private Config config;
   ```

2. The second way is to call the static method, `org.eclipse.microprofile.config.ConfigProvider#getConfig()`, to obtain an instance of `Config`:

   ```
   Config config = ConfigProvider.getConfig();
   ```

The `Config` interface provides two methods to retrieve properties:

- `getValue(String propertyName, Class propertyType)`: This method throws a runtime exception if the property is not present in the configuration. This method must be used only for **mandatory** configuration (the application would not be able to function properly in its absence).

- `getOptionalValue(String propertyName, Class propertyType)`: This method returns a `java.util.Optional` object that is empty if the property is not present in the configuration. This method is used for **optional** configuration.

Both methods will also throw exceptions if the property value, retrieved as `String` from the configuration, cannot be converted into the expected Java type passed as the second argument (converters are described in a later section).

In both methods, you need to specify the Java type you are expecting from the property. For example, if the property corresponds to a URL, you can get its value as `java.net.URL` directly:

```
URL myURL = config.getValue("my.url", URL.class);
```

The `Config` interface also defines methods to list config sources and all of the properties:

- `Iterable<String>getPropertyNames()` returns the names of the properties from all of the sources of configuration provided by the `Config` object.
- `Iterable<ConfigSource>getConfigSources()` returns all of the sources of configurations provided by the `Config` object.

# The @ConfigProperty annotation

The `@ConfigProperty` annotation can be used to inject configuration values in Java fields or method parameters using CDI, as shown:

```
@Inject
@ConfigProperty(name="my.url")
private URL myURL;
```

The `@ConfigProperty` annotation can have `defaultValue`, which is used to configure the field if the configuration property is not found in the underlying `Config`:

```
@Inject
@ConfigProperty(name="my.url", defaultValue="http://localhost/")
private URL myURL;
```

If `defaultValue` is not set and no property is found, the application will throw `DeploymentException` as it cannot be properly configured.

It is possible to use `Optional` if a configuration property might not be present, as shown in the following code block:

```
@Inject
@ConfigProperty(name="my.url")
private Optional<URL> someUrl; // will be set to Optional.empty if the
                               // property `my.url` cannot be found
```

After reading the configuration, we need to provide source configuration sources, which will be covered in the next section.

# Providing sources of configuration

The source of a configuration is represented by the ConfigSource interface. You do not need to implement this interface unless you want to provide a source of configurations that are not available by the MicroProfile implementation you use in your application.

If a property is found in multiple config sources, Config will return the value from the ConfigSource interface with the highest ordinal value.

Ordering ConfigSource is important as users can provide custom ConfigSource interfaces in addition to the default ones provided by the MicroProfile Config implementation.

## Default ConfigSources

By default, a MicroProfile Config implementation must provide three sources of configuration:

- System properties from the Java virtual machine (with an ordinal of 400)
- Environment variables (with an ordinal of 300)
- Properties stored in META-INF/microprofile-config.properties (with an ordinal of 100)

The ordinal value of a config source determines the precedence of the config source. In particular, if a property is defined both in the system properties and the environment variables, the value will be taken from the system properties (which has a higher ordinal than the environment variables).

There are no restrictions on the names of properties. However, some operating systems can impose some restrictions on the name of the environment variables (for example, "." is not allowed by most Unix shells). If you have a property that could be configured from the environment variables, you have to name your property accordingly.

For example, the property name my_url can be used by an environment variable while my.url cannot.

### New in MicroProfile Config 1.3

MicroProfile Config 1.3 introduces a mapping rule from the config property name to the environment variable. This rule searches three environment variable variants for each property name:

- Exact match
- Replace any non-alphanumeric character with _
- Replace any non-alphanumeric character with _ and use uppercase

This means that, in the Java application, we can have a property named app.auth.url and use the APP_AUTH_URL environment variable to configure it.

Let's move on to the other type of configuration source.

# Custom ConfigSources implementations

It is possible to provide additional sources of configuration in your application that will be automatically added by the MicroProfile Config implementation.

You need to define an implementation of org.eclipse.microprofile.config.spi.ConfigSource and add a Java ServiceLoader configuration for it, and put that file in your application archive as META-INF/services/org.eclipse.microprofile.config.spi.ConfigSource. For your reference, here is an example of the definition of an implementation of an environment ConfigSource:

```
package io.packt.sample.config;

import java.io.Serializable;
import java.util.Collections;
import java.util.Map;

import org.eclipse.microprofile.config.spi.ConfigSource;

public class EnvConfigSource implements ConfigSource, Serializable {

    EnvConfigSource() {
    }

    @Override
    public Map<String, String> getProperties() {
```

```
        return Collections.unmodifiableMap(System.getenv());
    }

    @Override
    public int getOrdinal() {
        return 300;
    }

    @Override
    public String getValue(String name) {
        if (name == null) {
            return null;
        }

        // exact match
        String value = System.getenv(name);
        if (value != null) {
            return value;
        }

        // replace non-alphanumeric characters by underscores
        name = name.replaceAll("[^a-zA-Z0-9_]", "_");

        value = System.getenv(name);
        if (value != null) {
            return value;
        }

        // replace non-alphanumeric characters by underscores and convert
        // to uppercase
        return System.getenv(name.toUpperCase());
    }

    @Override
    public String getName() {
        return "EnvConfigSource";
    }
}
```

In addition to providing additional ConfigSource, the MicroProfile Config API allows users to convert *raw* config property values into application-specific objects using converters, as described in the next section.

# Using converters for high-level configuration

MicroProfile Config will read Java `String` objects from its `ConfigSource`. However, it provides facilities to *convert* these `String` objects into more specific types in your application.

For example, the `myUrl` field we described previously is a `URL` object. The corresponding property, `my.url`, is read as a `String` object and then converted into a `URL` object before it is injected.

If the application uses the `Config` object, the MicroProfile Config implementation will also convert the `String` object into the type passed as the second argument of the `getValue` and `getOptionalValue` methods. This conversion can be done using different converter types: built-in, automatic, and custom. We will talk about them in detail now.

## Built-in converters

The MicroProfile Config implementation provides built-in converters for the primitive types (`boolean`, `int`, `long`, `byte`, `float`, and `double`) and their corresponding Java types (for example, `Integer`).

It also provides support for arrays in the property value using the `","` as the item separator. If the `","` must be part of an item, it must be escaped with a backslash `"\"`:

```
private String[] pets = config.getValue("myPets", String[].class)
```

If the value of the `myPets` property is dog,cat,dog\\,cat, the elements of the array stored in `pets` would be `{"dog", "cat", "dog,cat"}`.

## Automatic converters

MicroProfile Config also defines *automatic converters*. If a converter is not known for a given Java type, it will attempt to convert a `String` object into it using any one of the three different approaches:

- The Java type has a public constructor with a `String` parameter.
- It has a `public static valueOf(String)` method.
- It has a `public static parse(String)` method.

That's how the `my.url` property was converted from `String` into `URL` since the `java.net.URL` type has the `public URL(String)` constructor.

# Custom converters

If your application defines Java types that do not provide any of these three cases covered by the automatic converters, MicroProfile Config can still provide conversion using custom converters that extend the `org.eclipse.microprofile.config.spi.Converter` interface defined in the following:

```
public interface Converter<T> {
    /**
     * Configure the string value to a specified type
     * @param value the string representation of a property value.
     * @return the converted value or null
     *
     * @throws IllegalArgumentException if the value cannot be converted to
       the specified type.
     */
    T convert(String value);
```

You have to write an implementation of `org.eclipse.microprofile.config.spi.Converter`, then add its name to the `/META-INF/services/org.eclipse.microprofile.config.spi.Converter` file and put that file in your application archive. For your reference, here is an example of the implementation of a custom converter that supports a named number concept:

```
package io.packt.sample.config;

import org.eclipse.microprofile.config.spi.Converter;

public class NamedNumberConverter implements Converter<NamedNumber> {
    /**
     * Parses an assignment type of expression into a name and number value
     * @param value name=Number expression
     * @return NamedNumber instance
     */
    @Override
    public NamedNumber convert(String value) {
        String[] parts = value.split("="); // 1
        return new NamedNumber(parts[0], parts[1]);
    }
}

package io.packt.sample.config;

public class NamedNumber {
    private String name;
    private Number number;
```

```
public NamedNumber(String name, Number number) {
  this.name = name;
  this.number = number;
}

...
}
```

The converter takes a string and splits it based on a comma separator to extract the name and corresponding value to build the `NamedNumber` instance.

You would then specify a named number in your configuration, as shown here:

```
# microprofile-config.properties NamedNumber example
injected.namedNumber=jdoe,2.0
```

The addition of `NamedNumberConverter` allows us to use the `NamedNumber` type as a configuration type that can be injected. Here is an example that would match the configuration setting shown previously:

```
@Inject
@ConfigProperty(name="injected.namedNumber")
NamedNumber configuredNumber;
```

With the base MicroProfile Config feature covered, let's move onto another feature, MicroProfile Fault Tolerance.

# Understanding Eclipse MicroProfile Fault Tolerance

Fault Tolerance provides a collection of tools that prevent code from failing by making it more resilient. Most of these tools are inspired by development good practices (such as retry or fallback) or well-known development patterns (such as circuit breaker or bulkhead).

Fault Tolerance is based on CDI and, more precisely, on the CDI interceptor implementation. It also relies on the MicroProfile Config specification to allow external configuration for Fault Tolerance policies.

The main idea of the specification is to decouple business logic from Fault Tolerance boilerplate code. To achieve that, the specification defines interceptor-binding annotations to apply Fault Tolerance policies on a method execution or on a class (in that case, all class methods have the same policy).

Policies included in the Fault Tolerance specification are the following:

- **Timeout**: This is applied with the `@Timeout` annotation. It adds a timeout to the current operation.
- **Retry**: This is applied with the `@Retry` annotation. It adds retry behavior and allows its configuration on the current operation.
- **Fallback**: This is applied with the `@Fallback` annotation. It defines the code to execute, should the current operation fail.
- **Bulkhead**: This is applied with the `@Bulkhead` annotation. It isolates failures in the current operation to preserve the execution of other operations.
- **Circuit Breaker**: This is applied with the `@CircuitBreaker` annotation. It provides an automatic fast failing execution to prevent overloading the system.
- **Asynchronous**: This is applied with the `@Asynchronous` annotation. It makes the current operation asynchronous (that is, code will be invoked asynchronously).

Applying one or more of these policies is as easy as adding the required annotations on the method (or the class) for which you'd like to have these policies enabled. So, using Fault Tolerance is rather simple. But this simplicity doesn't prevent flexibility, thanks to all of the configuration parameters available for each policy.

Right now, the following vendors provide an implementation for the Fault Tolerance specification:

- Red Hat in Thorntail and Quarkus
- IBM in Open Liberty
- Payara in Payara Server
- Apache Safeguard for Hammock and TomEE
- KumuluzEE for KumuluzEE framework

All of these implementations support Fault Tolerance and hence support the same set of features that are described in the next section.

# MicroProfile Fault Tolerance in action

As we just discussed, the Fault Tolerance specification provides a set of annotations that you have to apply on a class or method to enforce Fault Tolerance policies. That being said, you have to keep in mind that these annotations are interceptors binding and hence are only usable on CDI beans. So, be careful to define your class as CDI beans before applying Fault Tolerance annotations on them or their methods.

In the following sections, you'll find usage examples for each Fault Tolerance annotation.

## The @Asynchronous policy

Making an operation asynchronous is as simple as the following:

```
@Asynchronous
public Future<Connection> service() throws InterruptedException {
  Connection conn = new Connection() {
    {
      Thread.sleep(1000);
    }

    @Override
    public String getData() {
      return "service DATA";
    }
  };
  return CompletableFuture.completedFuture(conn);
}
```

The only constraint is to have the @Asynchronous method return Future or CompletionStage; otherwise, the implementation should throw an exception.

## The @Retry policy

Should the operation fail, you can apply the retry policy to have the operation invoked again. The @Retry annotation can be used on a class or method level like this:

```
@Retry(maxRetries = 5, maxDuration= 1000, retryOn = {IOException.class})
public void operationToRetry() {
  ...
}
```

In the previous example, the operation should be retried a maximum of five times only on IOException. If the total duration of all retries lasts more than 1,000 ms, the operation will be aborted.

# The @Fallback policy

The @Fallback annotation can only be applied on a method; annotating a class will give an unexpected result:

```
@Retry(maxRetries = 2)
@Fallback(StringFallbackHandler.class)
public String shouldFallback() {
    ...
}
```

The fallback method is called after the number of retries is reached. In the previous example, the method will be retried twice in case of an error, and then the fallback will be used to invoke another piece of code—in this case, the following StringFallbackHandler class:

```
import javax.enterprise.context.ApplicationScoped;

import org.eclipse.microprofile.config.inject.ConfigProperty;
import org.eclipse.microprofile.faulttolerance.ExecutionContext;
import org.eclipse.microprofile.faulttolerance.FallbackHandler;

@ApplicationScoped
public class StringFallbackHandler implements FallbackHandler<String> {
    @ConfigProperty(name="app1.requestFallbackReply", defaultValue =
"Unconfigured Default Reply")
    private String replyString;

    @Override
    public String handle(ExecutionContext ec) {
        return replyString;
    }
}
```

Fallback code can be defined by a class implementing the FallbackHandler interface (see the previous code) or by a method in the current bean. In the StringFallbackHandler code, a MicroProfile Config property named app1.requestFallbackReply is used to externalize the application's fallback string value.

# The @Timeout policy

The @Timeout annotation could be applied to a class or method to make sure that an operation doesn't last forever:

```
@Timeout(200)
public void operationCouldTimeout() {
   ...
}
```

In the preceding example, the operation will be stopped should it last more than 200 ms.

# The @CircuitBreaker policy

The @CircuitBreaker annotation can be applied to a class or method. The circuit breaker pattern was introduced by Martin Fowler to protect the execution of an operation by making it fail fast in case of a dysfunction:

```
@CircuitBreaker(requestVolumeThreshold = 4, failureRatio=0.75, delay =
1000)
public void operationCouldBeShortCircuited(){
   ...
}
```

In the previous example, the method applies the CircuitBreaker policy. The circuit will be opened if three (*4 x 0.75*) failures occur among the rolling window of four consecutive invocations. The circuit will stay open for 1,000 ms and then be back to half-open. After a successful invocation, the circuit will be back to closed again.

# The @Bulkhead policy

The @Bulkhead annotation can also be applied to a class or method to enforce the bulkhead policy. This pattern isolates failures in the current operation to preserve the execution of other operations. The implementation does this by limiting the number of concurrent invocations on a given method:

```
@Bulkhead(4)
public void bulkheadedOperation() {
   ...
}
```

In the previous code, this method only supports four invocations at the same time. Should more than four simultaneous requests come into the `bulkheadedOperation` method, the system will hold the fifth and later requests until one of the four active invocations completes. The bulkhead annotation can also be used with `@Asynchronous` to limit the thread number in an asynchronous operation.

# Tolerance with MicroProfile config

As we saw in the previous sections, Fault Tolerance policies are applied by using annotations. For most use cases, this is enough, but for others, this approach may not be satisfactory because configuration is done at the source code level.

That's the reason why the parameters of MicroProfile Fault Tolerance annotations can be overridden using MicroProfile Config.

The annotation parameters can be overwritten via config properties using the following naming convention: `<classname>/<methodname>/<annotation>/<parameter>`.

To override `maxDuration` for `@Retry` on the `doSomething` method in the `MyService` class, set the config property like this:

```
org.example.microservice.MyService/doSomething/Retry/maxDuration=3000
```

If the parameters for a particular annotation need to be configured with the same value for a particular class, use the `<classname>/<annotation>/<parameter>` config property for configuration.

For instance, use the following config property to override all `maxRetries` for `@Retry` specified on the `MyService` class to 100:

```
org.example.microservice.MyService/Retry/maxRetries=100
```

Sometimes, the parameters need to be configured with the same value for the whole microservice (that is, all occurrences of the annotation in the deployment).

In this circumstance, the `<annotation>/<parameter>` config property overrides the corresponding parameter value for the specified annotation. For instance, to override all `maxRetries` for all of `@Retry` to be 30, specify the following config property:

```
Retry/maxRetries=30
```

This brings us to the end of discussion on Fault Tolerance in MicroProfile.

# Summary

In this chapter, we learned how to use MicroProfile Config to configure MicroProfile applications and MicroProfile Fault Tolerance to make them more resilient.

In MicroProfile Config, the sources of the configuration can be many; some values come from properties files and others from system properties or environment variables, but they are all accessed consistently from the Java application. The values will likely differ according to the deployment environment (for example, testing and production) but that is transparent in the application code.

MicroProfile Fault Tolerance helps to prevent failure in applications by applying specific policies in the code. It comes with default behavior but can be configured thanks to MicroProfile Config.

The next chapter will show how MicroProfile applications can provide information regarding their status (health) and how they can be secured thanks to MicroProfile JWT propagation.

# Questions

1. What are the default sources of configuration properties supported by MicroProfile Config?
2. What can you do if you need to integrate another source of configuration properties?
3. Are only the string type of properties supported?
4. Does injecting a configuration property into your code force you to provide a value for that property?
5. Suppose you have complex property types. Is there a way to integrate them into MicroProfile Config?
6. What happens when a Fault Tolerance annotation is applied to a class?
7. True or false: there are at least 10 different Fault Tolerance policies?
8. Does a `@Retry` policy require a retry on all failures?
9. Are we stuck with the Fault Tolerance annotation setting that is used in the application code?

# Further reading

Additional details for the MicroProfile Config feature can be found in the MicroProfile Config specification at `https://github.com/eclipse/microprofile-config/releases`. Additional details for the MicroProfile Fault Tolerance feature can be found in the MicroProfile Config specification at `https://github.com/eclipse/microprofile-config/releases`.

# 4
# MicroProfile Health Check and JWT Propagation

In this chapter, we will introduce the MicroProfile Health Check and **JSON Web Token (JWT)** Propagation projects. The Health Check project is concerned with exposing the application-defined health to the outside world, and JWT Propagation is concerned with defining an interoperable security token and use of that token in an application. In this chapter, you will learn the concerns that these specifications address, their constructs, and how to use them in your application. The code snippets throughout this chapter are for reference only. If you would like a working code version of this specification, please refer to `Chapter 8`, *A Working Eclipse MicroProfile Code Sample*.

We will cover the following topics:

- What a health check is
- How MicroProfile Health Check exposes the health check endpoint and the format of a query to that endpoint
- How to write a MicroProfile Health Check for your application
- The required format for the tokens in MicroProfile JWT Propagation
- How we can leverage MicroProfile JWT Propagation for security decisions

# Technical requirements

To build and run the samples in this chapter, you need Maven 3.5+ and a Java 8 JDK. The code for this chapter can be found at `https://github.com/PacktPublishing/Hands-On-Enterprise-Java-Microservices-with-Eclipse-MicroProfile/tree/master/Chapter04-healthcheck` and `https://github.com/PacktPublishing/Hands-On-Enterprise-Java-Microservices-with-Eclipse-MicroProfile/tree/master/Chapter04-jwtpropagation` for the MicroProfile Health Check and MicroProfile Propagation JWT sections, respectively.

# Understanding health checks and how MicroProfile handles them

In cloud-native architectures, health checks are used to determine whether a computing node is alive and ready to perform work. The concept of readiness describes the state when containers start up or roll over (that is, redeployment). During this time, the cloud platform needs to ensure that no network traffic is routed to that instance before it is ready to perform work.

Liveness, on the other hand, describes the state of a running container; that is, can it still respond to requests? If either the liveness or readiness states are seen as invalid, the computing node will be discarded (terminated or shut down) and eventually replaced by another, healthy, instance.

Health checks are an essential contract with the orchestration framework and scheduler of the cloud platform. The check procedures are provided by the application developer and the platform uses these to continuously ensure the availability of your application or service.

MicroProfile Health Check 1.0 (MP-HC) supports a single health check endpoint that can be utilized for either a liveness or readiness check. MicroProfile Health Check 2.0 plans to add support for multiple endpoints to allow an application to define both liveness and readiness probes.

The MP-HC specification details two elements: a protocol along with a response wire format part and a Java API for defining the response content.

The architecture of the MP-HC feature is modeled as an application that consists of zero or more health check procedures that are logically linked together with AND to derive the overall health check status. A procedure represents an application-defined check of a required condition that has a name, state, and, optionally, data about the check.

# The Health Check protocol and wire format

The MP-HC specification defines the requirement to support the HTTP GET requests against a logical /health REST endpoint that may return any one of the following codes to represent the endpoint's status:

- 200: It is up and healthy.
- 500: It is unhealthy due to an unknown error.
- 503: It is down and not ready to respond to requests.

Note that many cloud environments simply look at the request return code as either success or failure, so the differentiation between a 500 and 503 code may not be distinguishable.

The payload of a /health request must be a JSON object that matches the schema given in the following (for more information on the JSON schema syntax see http://jsonschema. net/#/).

Following is the JSON schema for MicroProfile Health Check responses:

```
{
  "$schema": "http://json-schema.org/draft-04/schema#",
  "type": "object",
  "properties": {
    "outcome": {
      "type": "string"
    },
    "checks": {
      "type": "array",
      "items": {
        "type": "object",
        "properties": {
          "name": {
            "type": "string"
          },
          "state": {
            "type": "string"
          },
          "data": {
            "type": "object",
            "properties": {
              "key": {
                "type": "string"
              },
              "value": {
                "type": "string|boolean|int"
              }
            }
```

```
            }
          }
        },
        "required": [
          "name",
          "state"
        ]
      }
    }
  },
  "required": [
    "outcome",
    "checks"
  ]
}
```

So, an MP-HC response consists of a JSON object that contains a `status` property of the string type and a `checks` property of the array of objects type. The `checks` array object type consists of a required `name` and `status` string, along with an optional `data` object that contains optional `key` and `value` pairs. In the next section, we will see how a microservice specifies a health check response.

# The Health Check Java API

Most of the plumbing is performed by the application framework that implements the MP-HC specification. Your part is to decide how liveness or readiness are determined through the health check procedures that your microservice defines using the MP-HC API.

To do this, you need to implement a health check procedure by implementing one or more instances of the `HealthCheck` interface using beans that are marked with a `Health` annotation.

The `HealthCheck` interface is provided in the following code block:

```
package org.eclipse.microprofile.health;

@FunctionalInterface
public interface HealthCheck {
  HealthCheckResponse call();
}
```

The code for the `Health` annotation is provided in the following code block:

```
package org.eclipse.microprofile.health;

import javax.inject.Qualifier;
import java.lang.annotation.Documented;
import java.lang.annotation.Retention;
import java.lang.annotation.RetentionPolicy;

@Qualifier
@Documented
@Retention(RetentionPolicy.RUNTIME)
public @interface Health {
}
```

An example `HealthCheck` implementation that represents the status of a hypothetical disk space check is shown in the following example. Note that the check includes the current free space as part of the response data. The `HealthCheckResponse` class supports a builder interface to populate the response object.

Following is a hypothetical disk space `HealthCheck` procedure implementation:

```
import javax.enterprise.context.ApplicationScoped;
import org.eclipse.microprofile.health.Health;
import org.eclipse.microprofile.health.HealthCheck;
import org.eclipse.microprofile.health.HealthCheckResponse;

@Health
@ApplicationScoped
public class CheckDiskspace implements HealthCheck {
  @Override
  public HealthCheckResponse call() {
      return HealthCheckResponse.named("diskspace")
              .withData("free", "780mb")
              .up()
              .build();
  }
}
```

In this example, we created a health response that is named `diskspace` with a status of `up` and custom data named `free` with a string value of `780mb`.

Another health check example representing some service endpoint is shown in the following.

A hypothetical service `HealthCheck` procedure implementation is shown here:

```
package io.packt.hc.rest;
//ServiceCheck example

import javax.enterprise.context.ApplicationScoped;
import org.eclipse.microprofile.health.Health;
import org.eclipse.microprofile.health.HealthCheck;
import org.eclipse.microprofile.health.HealthCheckResponse;

@Health
@ApplicationScoped
public class ServiceCheck implements HealthCheck {
 public HealthCheckResponse call() {
 return HealthCheckResponse.named("service-check")
 .withData("port", 12345)
 .withData("isSecure", true)
 .withData("hostname", "service.jboss.com")
 .up()
 .build();
 }
}
```

In this example, we created a health response named `service-check` with a status of `up` that includes the following additional data:

- A `port` item with an integer value of `12345`
- An `isSecure` item with a Boolean value of `true`
- A `hostname` item with a string value of `service.jboss.com`

The CDI-managed health checks are discovered and registered automatically by the application runtime. The runtime automatically exposes an HTTP endpoint, `/health`, used by the cloud platform to poke into your application to determine its state. You can test this by building the `Chapter04-healthcheck` application and running it. You will see the following output:

```
Scotts-iMacPro:hc starksm$ mvn package
[INFO] Scanning for projects...
. . .
Resolving 144 out of 420 artifacts

[INFO] Repackaging .war:
/Users/starksm/Dev/JBoss/Microprofile/PacktBook/Chapter04-
metricsandhc/hc/target/health-check.war

[INFO] Repackaged .war:
```

```
/Users/starksm/Dev/JBoss/Microprofile/PacktBook/Chapter04-
metricsandhc/hc/target/health-check.war

[INFO] ---------------------------------------------------------------
---

[INFO] BUILD SUCCESS

[INFO] ---------------------------------------------------------------
---

[INFO] Total time:  7.660 s

[INFO] Finished at: 2019-04-16T21:55:14-07:00

[INFO] ---------------------------------------------------------------
---

Scotts-iMacPro:hc starksm$ java -jar target/health-check-thorntail.jar

2019-04-16 21:57:03,305 INFO  [org.wildfly.swarm] (main) THORN0013:
Installed fraction: MicroProfile Fault Tolerance - STABLE
io.thorntail:microprofile-fault-tolerance:2.4.0.Final

...

2019-04-16 21:57:07,449 INFO  [org.jboss.as.server] (main) WFLYSRV0010:
Deployed "health-check.war" (runtime-name : "health-check.war")

2019-04-16 21:57:07,453 INFO  [org.wildfly.swarm] (main) THORN99999:
Thorntail is Ready
```

Once the server has started, test the health checks by querying the health endpoint:

```
Scotts-iMacPro:Microprofile starksm$ curl -s http://localhost:8080/health |
jq
{
 "outcome": "UP",
 "checks": [
   {
     "name": "service-check",
     "state": "UP",
     "data": {
       "hostname": "service.jboss.com",
       "port": 12345,
       "isSecure": true
     }
   },
```

```
    {
      "name": "diskspace",
      "state": "UP",
      "data": {
        "free": "780mb"
      }
    }
  ]
}
```

This shows the overall health to be UP. The overall status is the logical OR of all of the health check procedures found in the application. In this case, it is AND of the two health check procedures we have seen: diskspace and service-check.

# Integration with the cloud platform

Most cloud platforms support both TCP- and HTTP-based checks. To integrate health checks with your selected cloud platform, you need to configure your cloud deployment to point to the HTTP entry point, /health, on the node that hosts your application.

The cloud platform will invoke a GET query on the HTTP entry point; all checks that are registered will be performed and the sum of individual checks determines the overall outcome.

Usually, the response payload is ignored by the cloud platform and it only looks at the HTTP status code to determine the liveness or readiness of your application. A successful outcome, UP, will be mapped to 200 and DOWN to 503.

# Human operators

The primary use case for the JSON response payload is to provide a way for operators to investigate the application state. To support this, health checks allow for additional data to be attached to a health check response as we have seen in the CheckDiskspace and ServiceCheck examples. Consider the following fragment:

```
[...]
return HealthCheckResponse
        .named("memory-check")
        .withData("free-heap", "64mb")
        .up()
        .build();
[...]
```

Here, the additional information about `free-heap` is provided and will become part of the response payload, as shown in this response fragment. The JSON response fragment showing `memory-check` procedure content is as follows:

```
{
...
    "checks": [
        {
            "name": "memory-check",
            "state": "UP",
            "data": {
                "free-heap": "64mb"
            }
        }
    ],
    "outcome": "UP"
}
```

Here, we see the `memory-check` procedure with its `UP` state and additional `free-heap` data item of the string type with the value of `64mb`.

 **Eclipse resources/GitHub coordinates for MP-Health:**
The MP-Health project source code can be found at `https://github.com/eclipse/microprofile-health`.

# Changes in Health Check response messages

MicroProfile Health Check 3.0 introduced changes to the message format of health check JSON responses. Specifically, the field's outcome and state have been replaced by the field status.

In addition, the `@Health` qualifier was deprecated in the Health Check 3.0 release, while the `@Liveness` and `@Readiness` qualifiers were introduced. For the two qualifiers, the `/health/live` and `/health/ready` endpoints were also introduced to call all the liveliness and readiness procedures, respectively. Lastly, for backward compatibility, `/health` endpoint now calls all the procedures that have `@Health`, `@Liveness`, or `@Readiness` qualifiers.

It's time to discuss JWT Propagation now.

# Using JSON Web Token Propagation in MicroProfile

A **JSON Web Token (JWT)** is a common format for carrying security information that is used by many different web-based security protocols. However, there is a lack of standardization around exactly what the contents of the JWT are and what security algorithms are used with signed JWTs. The **MicroProfile JWT (MP-JWT)** Propagation project specification looked at the **OpenID Connect (OIDC)**-based (http://openid.net/connect/) JWT (https://tools.ietf.org/html/rfc7519) specifications and built upon those to define a set of requirements to promote interoperability of JWTs for use in MicroProfile-based microservices, along with APIs to access information from the JWTs.

 For a description of how OIDC and JWT work, including how an application/microservice intercepts bearer tokens, please refer to the *Basic Client Implementer's Guide* at http://openid.net/connect/.

In this section, you will learn about the following:

- The claims and signature algorithms from OIDC and JWT specifications that were required for interoperability
- Using JWTs for **Role-Based Access Control (RBAC)** of microservice endpoints
- How to use the MP-JWT APIs to access a JWT and its claim values

## Recommendations for interoperability

The maximum utility of MP-JWT as a token format depends on the agreement between both identity providers and service providers. This means identity providers—responsible for issuing tokens—should be able to issue tokens using the MP-JWT format in a way that service providers can understand to inspect the token and gather information about a subject. The primary goals for MP-JWT are as follows:

- It should be usable as an authentication token.
- It should be usable as an authorization token that contains application-level roles indirectly granted via a group's claim.
- It can support additional standard claims described in IANA JWT Assignments (https://www.iana.org/assignments/jwt/jwt.xhtml), as well as non-standard claims.

To meet those requirements, we introduced two new claims to the MP-JWT:

- `upn`: A human-readable claim that uniquely identifies the subject or user principal of the token, across the MicroProfile services with which the token will be accessed
- `groups`: The token subject's group memberships that will be mapped to RBAC-style application-level roles in the MicroProfile service container

# Required MP-JWT claims

The required set of MP-JWT claims for which an implementation needs to provide support contains the following:

- `typ`: This header parameter identifies the token type and is required to be `JWT`.
- `alg`: This header algorithm was used to sign the JWT and must be specified as `RS256`.
- `kid`: This header parameter provides a hint about which public key was used to sign the JWT.
- `iss`: This is the issuer and signer of the token.
- `sub`: This identifies the subject of the JWT.
- `exp`: This identifies the expiration time on, or after, which the JWT MUST NOT be accepted for processing.
- `iat`: This identifies the time at which the JWT was issued and can be used to determine the age of the JWT.
- `jti`: This provides a unique identifier for the JWT.
- `upn`: This MP-JWT custom claim is the preferred way to specify a user principal name.
- `groups`: This MP-JWT custom claim is the list of group or role names assigned to the JWT principal.

> `NumericDate` used by `exp`, `iat`, and other date-related claims is a JSON numeric value representing the number of seconds from `1970-01-01T00:00:00Z` UTC until the specified UTC date/time, ignoring leap seconds. Additionally, more details about the standard claims may be found in the MP-JWT specification (`https://github.com/eclipse/microprofile-jwt-auth/releases/tag/1.1.1`) and the JSON Web Token RFC (`https://tools.ietf.org/html/rfc7519`).

An example basic MP-JWT in JSON would be a sample header and payload of an MP-JWT compatible JWT, as shown here:

```
{
    "typ": "JWT",
    "alg": "RS256",
    "kid": "abc-1234567890"
}
{
    "iss": "https://server.example.com",
    "jti": "a-123",
    "exp": 1311281970,
    "iat": 1311280970,
    "sub": "24400320",
    "upn": "jdoe@server.example.com",
    "groups": ["red-group", "green-group", "admin-group", "admin"],
}
{
*** base64 signature not shown ***
}
```

This example shows the header with `typ=JWT`, `alg=RS256`, and `kid=abc-1234567890`. The body includes the `iss`, `jti`, `exp`, `iat`, `sub`, `upn`, and `groups` claims.

## The high-level description of the MP-JWT API

The MP-JWT project introduces the following API interfaces and classes under the `org.eclipse.microprofile.jwt` package namespace:

- `JsonWebToken`: This is a `java.security.Principal` interface extension that makes the set of required claims available via get-style accessors, along with general access to any claim in the JWT.
- `Claims`: This is an enumeration utility class that encapsulates all of the standard JWT-related claims along with a description and the required Java type for the claim as returned from the `JsonWebToken#getClaim(String)` method.
- `Claim`: This is a qualifier annotation used to signify an injection point for `ClaimValue`.
- `ClaimValue<T>`: This is a `java.security.Principal` interface extension for use with the `Claim` qualifier to directly inject claim values from the JWT.

There is an additional `org.eclipse.microprofile.auth.LoginConfig` annotation that is used to define security context information such as the realm name and authentication mechanism name. This is needed because MicroProfile does not specify a deployment format and currently does not rely on servlet metadata descriptors. The `LoginConfig` annotation provides the same information as `web.xml login-config` element.

Before we start looking at code samples, the following screenshot is an exploded view of this chapter's source code layout. It will help you to understand where the files are located as we reference them in subsequent examples:

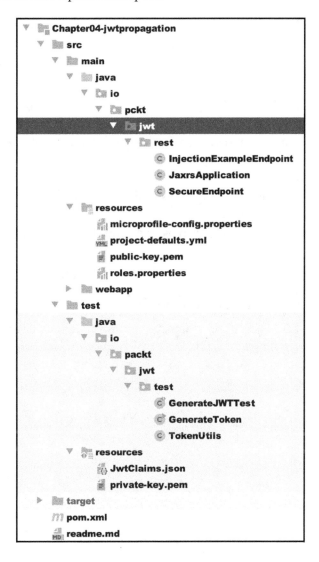

Its intended usage is to mark a JAX-RS application as requiring MicroProfile JWT RBAC, as shown in the following sample:

```
package io.pckt.jwt.rest;

import javax.ws.rs.ApplicationPath;
import javax.ws.rs.core.Application;
import org.eclipse.microprofile.auth.LoginConfig;

@LoginConfig(authMethod = "MP-JWT", realmName = "Packt")
@ApplicationPath("/")
public class JaxrsApplication extends Application {
}
```

For security constraint declarations, MP-JWT implementations rely on the Java(TM) Common Annotations security annotations found in the `javax.annotation.security` package. The annotations that MP-JWT implementations must support include the following:

- `DenyAll`: It marks that no access is allowed regardless of the roles contained in the JWT. This is often used as the class level to specify a default behavior that disallows access.
- `PermitAll`: It marks that all access is allowed, including unauthenticated access that includes no JWT information.
- `RolesAllowed`: It defines the roles and groups that are required to be granted to the JWT for access to the endpoint.

## Sample code that uses MP-JWT

The basic usage of the MP-JWT API is to inject `JsonWebToken`, its `ClaimValue`, or both. In this section, we present snippets of typical usage. This book's code for this section is available at `https://github.com/PacktPublishing/Hands-On-Enterprise-Java-Microservices-with-Eclipse-MicroProfile/tree/master/Chapter04-jwtpropagation`.

# Injection of JsonWebToken information

The following code sample illustrates access of the incoming MP-JWT token as `JsonWebToken`, the raw JWT token string, the `upn` claim, and integration with JAX-RS `SecurityContext`:

```
package io.pckt.jwt.rest;

import javax.annotation.security.DenyAll;
import javax.annotation.security.PermitAll;
import javax.annotation.security.RolesAllowed;
import javax.inject.Inject;
import javax.ws.rs.GET;
import javax.ws.rs.Path;
import javax.ws.rs.Produces;
import javax.ws.rs.core.Context;
import javax.ws.rs.core.MediaType;
import javax.ws.rs.core.SecurityContext;
import org.eclipse.microprofile.jwt.Claim;
import org.eclipse.microprofile.jwt.Claims;
import org.eclipse.microprofile.jwt.JsonWebToken;

@Path("/jwt")
@DenyAll //1
public class SecureEndpoint {
    @Inject
 private JsonWebToken jwt; //2
    @Inject
    @Claim(standard = Claims.raw_token)
    private String jwtString; //3

    @Inject
    @Claim(standard = Claims.upn)
    private String upn; //4

    @Context
    private SecurityContext context; //5

    @GET
    @Path("/openHello")
    @Produces(MediaType.TEXT_PLAIN)
    @PermitAll //6
    public String openHello() {
        String user = jwt == null ? "anonymous" : jwt.getName();
        String upnClaim = upn == null ? "no-upn" : upn;
        return String.format("Hello[open] user=%s, upn=%s", user,
        upnClaim);
    }
```

```
@GET
@Path("/secureHello")
@Produces(MediaType.TEXT_PLAIN)
@RolesAllowed("User") //7
public String secureHello() {
    String user = jwt == null ? "anonymous" : jwt.getName();
    String scheme = context.getAuthenticationScheme(); //8
    boolean isUserRole = context.isUserInRole("User"); //9
    return String.format("Hello[secure] user=%s, upn=%s, scheme=%s,
    isUserRole=%s", user, upn, scheme, isUserRole);
}
}
```

Let's discuss the commented notations:

1. The class level `DenyAll` annotation marks that the default access to the endpoints is to disallow any access.
2. This is the direct injection of the `JsonWebToken` interface view of the JWT.
3. This is the injection of the raw JWT token string. This could be used to propagate the incoming token in a chained call.
4. This is the injection of the `upn` claim value.
5. This is the JAX-RS `SecurityContext` interface. This integrates with the MP-JWT layer to provide access to the principal form of the JWT as well as its RBAC information.
6. The `PermitAll` annotation indicates that any caller, regardless of authentication status, can access the `/jwt/openHello` endpoint.
7. The `RolesAllowed` annotation indicates that the caller must have a `User` role assigned to access the `/jwt/secureHello` endpoint.
8. The `SecurityContext#getAuthenticationScheme` method is called to check the deployment authentication scheme. This should match `MP-JWT` from the `LoginConfig` annotation on the application class.
9. The `SecurityContext#isUserInRole(String)` method is called to illustrate that programmatic access to the JWT `groups` information integrates with the JAX-RS security layer.

## Injection of JWT claim values

The code snippet in this section illustrates the injection of individual JWT claim values. There are several different formats we can use for the injected value. Standard claims support the object subtypes defined in the `Claim#getType` field and `JsonValue` subtypes. Custom claim types only support the injection of the `JsonValue` subtypes.

The following code example illustrates injection of the standard `groups` and `iss` claims, along with `customString`, `customInteger`, `customDouble`, and `customObject` custom claims:

```java
package io.pckt.jwt.rest;

import java.util.Set;
import javax.annotation.security.DenyAll;
import javax.annotation.security.RolesAllowed;
import javax.inject.Inject;
import javax.json.JsonArray;
import javax.json.JsonNumber;
import javax.json.JsonObject;
import javax.json.JsonString;
import javax.ws.rs.GET;
import javax.ws.rs.Path;

import org.eclipse.microprofile.jwt.Claim;
import org.eclipse.microprofile.jwt.Claims;

@Path("/jwt")
@DenyAll
public class InjectionExampleEndpoint {
    @Inject
    @Claim(standard = Claims.groups)
    Set<String> rolesSet; // 1
    @Inject
    @Claim(standard = Claims.iss)
    String issuer; // 2

    @Inject
    @Claim(standard = Claims.groups)
    JsonArray rolesAsJson; // 3
    @Inject
    @Claim(standard = Claims.iss)
    JsonString issuerAsJson; // 4
    // Custom claims as JsonValue types
    @Inject
    @Claim("customString")
    JsonString customString; // 5
    @Inject
    @Claim("customInteger")
    JsonNumber customInteger; // 6
    @Inject
    @Claim("customDouble")
    JsonNumber customDouble; // 7
    @Inject
    @Claim("customObject")
```

```
    JsonObject customObject; // 8

    @GET
    @Path("/printClaims")
    @RolesAllowed("Tester")
    public String printClaims() {
        return String.format("rolesSet=%s\n");
    }
}
```

The eight commented injections are as follows:

1. Injection of the standard `groups` claim as its default `Set<String>` type
2. Injection of the standard `iss` claim as its default String type
3. Injection of the standard `groups` claim as its default `JsonArray` type
4. Injection of the standard `iss` claim as its default `JsonString` type
5. Injection of a non-standard `customString` claim as a `JsonString` type
6. Injection of a non-standard `customInteger` claim as a `JsonNumber` type
7. Injection of a non-standard `customDouble` claim as a `JsonNumber` type
8. Injection of a non-standard `customObject` claim as a `JsonString` type

# Configuring authentication of JWTs

To accept a JWT as representing an identity that should be authenticated and therefore trusted, we need to configure the MP-JWT feature with the information to verify who signed and who issued the JWT. This is done via MP-Config properties:

- `mp.jwt.verify.publickey`: This provides the embedded key material of the public key for the MP-JWT signer, typically in PKCS8 PEM format.
- `mp.jwt.verify.issuer`: This specifies the expected value of the `iss` claim found in the JWT.

An example `microprofile-configuration.properties` file for this book is as follows:

```
# MP-JWT Config
mp.jwt.verify.publickey=MIIBIjANBgkqhkiG9w0BAQEFAAOCAQ8AMIIBCgKCAQEAlivFI8q
B4D0y2jy0CfEqFyy46R0o7S8TKpsx5xbHKoU1VWg6QkQm+ntyIv1p4kE1sPEQO73+HY8+Bzs75X
wRTYL1BmR1w8J5hmjVWjc6R2BTBGAYRPFRhor3kpM6ni2SPmNNhurEAHw7TaqszP5eUF/F9+KEB
WkwVta+PZ37bwqSE4sCb1soZFrVz/UT/LF4tYpuVYt3YbqToZ3pZOZ9AX2o1GCG3xwOjkc4x0W7
ezbQZdC9iftPxVHR8irOijJRRjcPDtA6vPKpzL16CyYnsIYPd99ltwxTHjr3npfv/3Lw50bAkbT
4HeLFxTx4flEoZLKO/g0bAoV2uqBhkA9xnQIDAQAB
mp.jwt.verify.issuer=http://io.packt.jwt
```

The complete process of authenticating an MP-JWT is as follows:

1. Verify that the JWT has a valid header indicating the JWT was signed using the RS256 algorithm.
2. Verify that the JWT is signed correctly using the public key provided via the `mp.jwt.verify.publickey` setting.
3. Verify that the `JWT#iss` claim matches the `mp.jwt.verify.issuer` setting.
4. Verify that the JWT is not expired

# Running the samples

The samples we looked at can be deployed to Thorntail and accessed via command-line queries against the endpoints to validate the expected behaviors. Since authentication against the endpoints marked with security constraints requires a valid JWT, we need a way to generate a JWT that will be accepted by the Thorntail server.

This chapter's code provides an `io.packt.jwt.test.GenerateToken` utility that will create a JWT signed by a key that has been configured with the Thorntail server. The claims included in the JWT are defined by the `src/test/resources/JwtClaims.json` document of this chapter's project. You run the utility using the `mvn exec:java` command, as shown here:

```
Scotts-iMacPro:jwtprop starksm$ mvn exec:java -
Dexec.mainClass=io.packt.jwt.test.GenerateToken -Dexec.classpathScope=test
[INFO] Scanning for projects...
[INFO]
[INFO] -----------------< io.microprofile.jwt:jwt-propagation >--------------
----
[INFO] Building JWT Propagation 1.0-SNAPSHOT
[INFO] --------------------------------[ war ]---------------------------------
----
[INFO]
[INFO] --- exec-maven-plugin:1.6.0:java (default-cli) @ jwt-propagation ---
Setting exp: 1555684338 / Fri Apr 19 07:32:18 PDT 2019
    Added claim: sub, value: 24400320
    Added claim: customIntegerArray, value: [0,1,2,3]
    Added claim: customDoubleArray, value: [0.1,1.1,2.2,3.3,4.4]
    Added claim: iss, value: http://io.packt.jwt
    Added claim: groups, value:
    ["Echoer","Tester","User","group1","group2"]
    Added claim: preferred_username, value: jdoe
    Added claim: customStringArray, value: ["value0","value1","value2"]
    Added claim: aud, value: [s6BhdRkqt3]
    Added claim: upn, value: jdoe@example.com
```

```
    Added claim: customInteger, value: 123456789
    Added claim: auth_time, value: 1555683738
    Added claim: customObject, value: {"my-service":{"roles":["role-in-my-
    service"],"groups":["group1","group2"]},"service-B":{"roles":["role-in-
    B"]},"service-C":{"groups":["groupC","web-tier"]},"scale":0.625}
    Added claim: exp, value: Fri Apr 19 07:32:18 PDT 2019
    Added claim: customDouble, value: 3.141592653589793
    Added claim: iat, value: Fri Apr 19 07:22:18 PDT 2019
    Added claim: jti, value: a-123
    Added claim: customString, value: customStringValue
```

```
eyJraWQiOiJcL3ByaXZhdGUta2V5LnBlbSIsInR5cCI6IkpXVCIsImFsZyI6IlJTMjU2In0.eyJ
zdWIiOiIyNDQwMDMyMCIsImN1c3RvbUludGVnZXJBcnJheSI6WzAsMSwyLDNdLCJjdXN0b21Eb3
VibGVBcnJheSI6WzAuMSwxLjEsMi4yLDMuMyw0LjRdLCJpc3MiOiJodHRwOlwvXC9pby55YWNrd
C5qd3QiLCJncm91cHMiOlsiRWNob2VyIiwiVGVzdGVyIiwiVXNlciIsImdyb3VwMSIsImdyb3Vw
MiJdLCJwcmVmZXJyZWRfdXNlcm5hbWUiOiJqZG91IiwiY3VzdG9tU3RyaW5nQXJyYXkiOlsidmF
sdWUwIiwidmFsdWUxIiwidmFsdWUyIl0sImF1ZCI6InM2QmhkUmtxdDMiLCJ1cG4iOiJqZG91QG
V4YW1wbGUuY29tIiwiY3VzdG9tSW50ZWdlciI6MTIzNDU2Nzg5LCJhdXRoX3RpbWUiOjE1NTU2O
DM3MzgsImN1c3RvbU9iamVjdCI6eyJteS1zZXJ2aWNlIjp7InJvbGVzIjpbInJvbGUtaW4tbXkt
c2Vydmlj ZSJdLCJncm91cHMiOlsiZ3JvdXAxIiwiZ3JvdXAyIl19LCJzZXJ2aWNlLUIiOnsicm9
sZXMiOlsicm9sZS1pbi1CIl19LCJzZXJ2aWNlLUMiOnsiЗ3JvdXBzIjpbImdyb3VwQyIsIndlYi
10aWVyIl19LCJzY2FsZSI6MC42MjV9LCJleHAiOjE1NTU2ODQzMzgsImN1c3RvbURvdWJsZSI6M
y4xNDE1OTI2NTM1ODk3OTMsImlhdCI6MTU1NTY4MzczOCwianRpIjoiYS0xMjMiLCJjdXN0b21T
dHJpbmciOiJjdXN0b21TdHJpbmdWYWx1ZSJ9.bF7CnutcQnA2gTlCRNOp4QMmWTWhwP86cSiPCS
xWr8N36FG79YC9Lx0Ugr-Ioo2Zw35z0Z0xEwjAQdKkkKYU9_1GsXiJgfYqzWS-
XxEtwhiinDOhUK2qiBcEHcY-ETx-
bsJud8_mSlrzEvrJEeX58Xy1Om1FxnjuiqmfBJxNaotxECScDcDMMH-DeA1Z-
nrJ3-0sdKNW6QxOxoR_RNrpci1F9y4pg-
eYOd8zE4tN_QbT3KkdMm91xPhv7QkKm71pnHxC0H4SmQJVEAX6bxdD51Az1NYrEMAJyyEgKuJeH
TxH8qzM-0FQHzrG3Yhnxax2x3Xd-6JtEbU-_E_3HRxvvw
```

```
[INFO] --------------------------------------------------------------------
----
[INFO] BUILD SUCCESS
[INFO] --------------------------------------------------------------------
----
[INFO] Total time:  1.339 s
[INFO] Finished at: 2019-04-19T07:22:19-07:00
[INFO] --------------------------------------------------------------------
----
```

The utility outputs the claims that were added and then prints out the base64-encoded JWT. You would use this JWT as the value in the `Authorization: Bearer` ... header of the `curl` command line you used to access the server endpoints.

To start up the Thorntail server with the example endpoints, cd into the Chapter04-jwtpropagation project directory and then run mvn to build the executable JAR:

```
Scotts-iMacPro:jwtprop starksm$ mvn package
[INFO] Scanning for projects...
[INFO]
[INFO] ----------------< io.microprofile.jwt:jwt-propagation >--------------
----
[INFO] Building JWT Propagation 1.0-SNAPSHOT
...
[INFO] ----------------------------------------------------------------------
----
[INFO] BUILD SUCCESS
[INFO] ----------------------------------------------------------------------
----
[INFO] Total time:  8.457 s
[INFO] Finished at: 2019-04-19T08:25:09-07:00
[INFO] ----------------------------------------------------------------------
----
```

The resulting executable JAR is located at target/jwt-propagation-thorntail.jar. You start up the Thorntail server with this chapter's sample deployment using java -jar ...:

```
Scotts-iMacPro:jwtprop starksm$ java -jar target/jwt-propagation-
thorntail.jar
2019-04-19 08:27:33,425 INFO  [org.wildfly.swarm] (main) THORN0013:
Installed fraction: MicroProfile Fault Tolerance - STABLE
io.thorntail:microprofile-fault-tolerance:2.4.0.Final
2019-04-19 08:27:33,493 INFO  [org.wildfly.swarm] (main) THORN0013:
Installed fraction:           Bean Validation - STABLE io.thorntail:bean-
validation:2.4.0.Final
2019-04-19 08:27:33,493 INFO  [org.wildfly.swarm] (main) THORN0013:
Installed fraction:      MicroProfile Config - STABLE
io.thorntail:microprofile-config:2.4.0.Final
2019-04-19 08:27:33,493 INFO  [org.wildfly.swarm] (main) THORN0013:
Installed fraction:            Transactions - STABLE
io.thorntail:transactions:2.4.0.Final
2019-04-19 08:27:33,494 INFO  [org.wildfly.swarm] (main) THORN0013:
Installed fraction:       CDI Configuration - STABLE io.thorntail:cdi-
config:2.4.0.Final
2019-04-19 08:27:33,494 INFO  [org.wildfly.swarm] (main) THORN0013:
Installed fraction: MicroProfile JWT RBAC Auth - STABLE
io.thorntail:microprofile-jwt:2.4.0.Final
...
2019-04-19 08:27:37,708 INFO  [org.jboss.as.server] (main) WFLYSRV0010:
Deployed "jwt-propagation.war" (runtime-name : "jwt-propagation.war")
```

```
2019-04-19 08:27:37,713 INFO  [org.wildfly.swarm] (main) THORN99999:
Thorntail is Ready
```

At this point, we can query the server endpoints. There is one endpoint that we defined that does not require any authentication. This is the `jwt/openHello` endpoint of the `io.pckt.jwt.rest.SecureEndpoint` class. Run the following command to validate that your Thorntail server is running as expected:

```
Scotts-iMacPro:jwtprop starksm$ curl http://localhost:8080/jwt/openHello;
echo
Hello[open] user=anonymous, upn=no-upn
```

Next, try the secured endpoint. It should fail with a **401 Not authorized** error because we are not providing any authorization information:

```
Scotts-iMacPro:jwtprop starksm$ curl http://localhost:8080/jwt/secureHello;
echo
Not authorized
```

Now, we need to generate a fresh JWT and pass that along with the curl command in the `Authorization` header, so let's try that. We will save the JWT generated by the mvn command in a JWT environment variable to simplify the curl command line:

```
Scotts-iMacPro:jwtprop starksm$ mvn exec:java -
Dexec.mainClass=io.packt.jwt.test.GenerateToken -Dexec.classpathScope=test
[INFO] Scanning for projects...
[INFO]
[INFO] ----------------< io.microprofile.jwt:jwt-propagation >--------------
----
[INFO] Building JWT Propagation 1.0-SNAPSHOT
[INFO] ------------------------------[ war ]-------------------------------
----
[INFO]
[INFO] --- exec-maven-plugin:1.6.0:java (default-cli) @ jwt-propagation ---
Setting exp: 1555688712 / Fri Apr 19 08:45:12 PDT 2019
    Added claim: sub, value: 24400320
    Added claim: customIntegerArray, value: [0,1,2,3]
    Added claim: customDoubleArray, value: [0.1,1.1,2.2,3.3,4.4]
    Added claim: iss, value: http://io.packt.jwt
    Added claim: groups, value:
    ["Echoer","Tester","User","group1","group2"]
    Added claim: preferred_username, value: jdoe
    Added claim: customStringArray, value: ["value0","value1","value2"]
    Added claim: aud, value: [s6BhdRkqt3]
    Added claim: upn, value: jdoe@example.com
    Added claim: customInteger, value: 123456789
    Added claim: auth_time, value: 1555688112
```

```
    Added claim: customObject, value: {"my-service":{"roles":["role-in-my-
    service"],"groups":["group1","group2"]},"service-B":{"roles":["role-in-
    B"]},"service-C":{"groups":["groupC","web-tier"]},"scale":0.625}
    Added claim: exp, value: Fri Apr 19 08:45:12 PDT 2019
    Added claim: customDouble, value: 3.141592653589793
    Added claim: iat, value: Fri Apr 19 08:35:12 PDT 2019
    Added claim: jti, value: a-123
    Added claim: customString, value: customStringValue
eyJraWQiOiJ...
[INFO] ------------------------------------------------------------------------
----
[INFO] BUILD SUCCESS
[INFO] ------------------------------------------------------------------------
----
[INFO] Total time:  1.352 s
[INFO] Finished at: 2019-04-19T08:35:12-07:00
[INFO] ------------------------------------------------------------------------
----
Scotts-iMacPro:jwtprop starksm$ JWT="eyJraWQiOi..."
Scotts-iMacPro:jwtprop starksm$ curl -H "Authorization: Bearer $JWT"
http://localhost:8080/jwt/secureHello; echo
Hello[secure] user=jdoe@example.com, upn=jdoe@example.com, scheme=MP-JWT,
isUserRole=true
```

> In the previous code snippet, for Windows users, please install a bash-compatible shell for Windows; otherwise, you will get an error due to the echo command.

This time, the query succeeds and we see that the username, upn claim value, scheme, and isUserInRole("User") check are as expected.

Now, try accessing the /jwt/printClaims endpoint that illustrated the injection of standard and non-standard claims as different types:

```
Scotts-iMacPro:jwtprop starksm$ curl -H "Authorization: Bearer $JWT"
http://localhost:8080/jwt/printClaims
+++ Standard claims as primitive types
rolesSet=[Echoer, Tester, User, group2, group1]
issuer=http://io.packt.jwt
+++ Standard claims as JSON types
rolesAsJson=["Echoer","Tester","User","group2","group1"]
issuerAsJson="http://io.packt.jwt"
+++ Custom claim JSON types
customString="customStringValue"
customInteger=123456789
customDouble=3.141592653589793
```

```
customObject={"my-service":{"roles":["role-in-my-
service"],"groups":["group1","group2"]},"service-B":{"roles":["role-in-
B"]},"service-C":{"groups":["groupC","web-tier"]},"scale":0.625}
```

Note that, if you begin to experience `Not authorized` errors after a while, the problem is that the JWT has expired. You either need to generate a new token or generate a token with a longer expiration. You can do this by passing in the expiration in seconds to the `GenerateToken` utility. For example, to generate a token that is valid for a full hour's use, perform the following:

```
Scotts-iMacPro:jwtprop starksm$ mvn exec:java -
Dexec.mainClass=io.packt.jwt.test.GenerateToken -Dexec.classpathScope=test
-Dexec.args="3600"
[INFO] Scanning for projects...
[INFO]
[INFO] ----------------< io.microprofile.jwt:jwt-propagation >--------------
----
[INFO] Building JWT Propagation 1.0-SNAPSHOT
[INFO] -------------------------------[ war ]-------------------------------
----
[INFO]
[INFO] --- exec-maven-plugin:1.6.0:java (default-cli) @ jwt-propagation ---
Setting exp: 1555692188 / Fri Apr 19 09:43:08 PDT 2019
    Added claim: sub, value: 24400320
    Added claim: customIntegerArray, value: [0,1,2,3]
    Added claim: customDoubleArray, value: [0.1,1.1,2.2,3.3,4.4]
    Added claim: iss, value: http://io.packt.jwt
    Added claim: groups, value:
["Echoer","Tester","User","group1","group2"]
    Added claim: preferred_username, value: jdoe
    Added claim: customStringArray, value: ["value0","value1","value2"]
    Added claim: aud, value: [s6BhdRkqt3]
    Added claim: upn, value: jdoe@example.com
    Added claim: customInteger, value: 123456789
    Added claim: auth_time, value: 1555688588
    Added claim: customObject, value: {"my-service":{"roles":["role-in-my-
service"],"groups":["group1","group2"]},"service-B":{"roles":["role-in-
B"]},"service-C":{"groups":["groupC","web-tier"]},"scale":0.625}
    Added claim: exp, value: Fri Apr 19 09:43:08 PDT 2019
    Added claim: customDouble, value: 3.141592653589793
    Added claim: iat, value: Fri Apr 19 08:43:08 PDT 2019
    Added claim: jti, value: a-123
    Added claim: customString, value: customStringValue
```

```
eyJraWQiOiJcL3ByaXZhdGUta2V5LnBlbSIsInR5cCI6IkpXVCIsImFsZyI6IlJTMjU2In0.eyJ
zdWIiOiIyNDQwMDMyMCIsImN1c3RvbUludGVnZXJBcnJheSI6WzAsMSwyLDNdLCJjdXN0b21Eb3
VibGVBcnJheSI6WzAuMSwxLjEsMi4yLDMuMyw0LjRdLCJpc3MiOiJodHRwOlwvXC9pby5wYWNrd
C5qd3QiLCJncm91cHMiOlsiRWNob2VyIiwiVGVzdGVyIiwiVXNlciIsImdyb3VwMSIsImdyb3Vw
```

MiJdLCJwcmVmZXJyZWRfdXNlcm5hbWUiOiJqZG9lIiwiY3VzdG9tU3RyaW5nQXJyYXkiOlsidmF
sdWUwIiwidmFsdWUxIiwidmFsdWUyIl0sImF1ZCI6InM2QmhkUmtxdDMiLCJ1c3Q4iOiJqZG91QG
V4YW1wbGUuY29tIiwiY3VzdG9tSW50ZWdlciI6MTIzNDU2Nzg5LCJhdXRoX3RpbWUiOjE1NTU2O
Dg1ODgsImNsc3RvbU9iamVjdCI6eyJteS5zZXJ2aWN1Ijp7InJvbGVzIjpbInJvbGUtaW4tbXkt
c2VydmljZSJdLCJncm91cHMiOlsiZ3JvdXAxIiwiZ3JvdXAyIl19LCJzZXJ2aWN1LUIiOnsicm9
sZXMiOlsicm9sZS1pbi1CIl19LCJzZXJ2aWN1LUMiOnsiZ3JvdXBzIjpbImdyb3VwQyIsIndlYi
10aWVyIl19LCJzc2FsZSI6MC42MjV9LCJleHAiOjE1NTU2OTIxODgsImN1c3RvbURvdWJsZSI6M
y4xNDE1OTI2NTM1ODk3OTMsImlhdCI6MTU1NTY4ODU4OCwianRpIjoiYS0xMjEiLCJjdXN0b21T
dHJpbmciOiJjdXN0b21TdHJpbmdWYWx1ZSJ9.Tb8Fet_3NhABc6E5z5N6afwNsxzcZaa9q0eWWL
m1AP4HPbJCOA14L275D-
jAO42s7yQlHS7sUsi9_nWStDV8MTqoey4PmN2rcnOAaKqCfUiLehcOzg3naUk0AxRykCBO4YIck
-
qqvlEaZ6q8pVW_2Nfj5wZml2uPDq_X6aVLfxjaRzj2F4OoeKGH51-88yeu7H2THUMNLLPB2MY4M
a0xDUFXVL1TXU49ilOXOWTHAo7wAdqleuZUavtt_ZQfRwCUoI1Y-
dltH_WtLdjjYw6aFIeJtsyYCXdqONiP6TqOpfACOXbV_nBYNKpYGn4GMiPsxmpJMU8JAhm-
jJzf9Yhq6A
```
[INFO] ----------------------------------------------------------------
---
[INFO] BUILD SUCCESS
[INFO] ----------------------------------------------------------------
---
[INFO] Total time:  1.328 s
[INFO] Finished at: 2019-04-19T08:43:08-07:00
[INFO] ----------------------------------------------------------------
---
```

These samples should give you a feel for the interaction between the microservice client and how the use of JWTs to secure microservice endpoints allows for stateless authentication and RBAC, as well as custom authorization based on claims in the JWT.

# Summary

In this chapter, we learned about the MicroProfile Health Check and JWT Propagation projects. You should now understand what a health check is and how to add application-specific checks, known as procedures. These allow your microservice to describe its non-trivial health requirements in a cloud environment. You should also understand how JWTs can be used to provide an authentication and authorization capability on top of your microservices to control access to your endpoints. You should also understand how content from the JWT can be used to augment your microservice in user-specific ways.

The next chapter will introduce the MicroProfile Metrics and OpenTracing features. These allow your microservices to provide additional information regarding common and application metrics and to trace the interactions between microservices.

# Questions

1. Is the MP-HC wire format useful in all environments?
2. Can an MP-HC response contain arbitrary properties?
3. What if my application has different types of services that need to report health status?
4. What is a JWT?
5. What is a claim?
6. Are there restrictions on what can be in a JWT?
7. What is/are the main step(s) in authenticating a JWT?
8. Beyond the security annotations, how might we perform an authorization check using JWTs?

# 5
# MicroProfile Metrics and OpenTracing

Once developers have written code and it is put into production, there is a need to observe what the code is doing, how well it is performing, and what resources it is using. MicroProfile has created two specifications to deal with these concerns: Metrics and (integration with) OpenTracing.

Starting off with the Metrics section, we will discuss the following topics:

- The rationale behind specifications
- Exposition formats of metrics on an enabled server
- Providing metrics from within your application
- Using Prometheus, a cloud-native time series database, to retrieve and analyze metric data

In the OpenTracing section, we will discuss the following:

- An introduction to the tracing domain
- Configuration properties
- Automatic and explicit tracing
- Showing data in the Jaeger tracing system

## MicroProfile Metrics

MicroProfile Metrics exposes the metric data (often called **telemetry**) of the running server, for example, CPU and memory usage, and the thread count. This data is then often fed into charting systems to visualize metrics over time or to serve capacity-planning purposes; of course, they also serve to notify DevOps people when the values go outside a predefined threshold range.

The Java Virtual Machine had a way to expose data for a long time via MBeans and the MBeanServer. Java SE 6 saw the introduction of an (RMI-based) remote protocol for all VMs defining how to access the MBean Server from remote processes. Dealing with this protocol is difficult and does not fit in with today's HTTP-based interactions.

The other pain point is that many globally existing servers have different properties exposed under different names. It is thus not easy to set up monitoring of different kinds of server.

MicroProfile has created a monitoring specification that addresses these two points via an HTTP-based API permitting access by monitoring agents and a Java API that allows application-specific metrics to be exported on top of a set of servers and JVM metrics.

 MicroProfile Metrics is developing the 2.x version of the specification that has some breaking changes to 1.x. The following sections talk about 1.x – the changes in 2.0 are discussed in the *New in MP-Metrics 2.0* section.

The specification defines three scopes for metrics:

- Base: These are metrics, mostly JVM statistics, that every compliant vendor has to support.
- Vendor: Optional vendor-specific metrics that are not portable.
- Application: Optional metrics from deployed applications. The Java API will be shown in the *Supplying application-specific metrics* section.

Another issue with the classic JMX approach, which MicroProfile Metrics addresses, is the lack of metadata information about the semantics of a metric.

# Metadata

Metadata is a very important part of MicroProfile Metrics. While it is possible to expose a metric `foo` with a value of `142`, it is not self-describing. An operator seeing that metric can't tell what this is about, what the unit is, and whether `142` is a good value or not.

Metadata is used to provide units and also a description of the metric so that the preceding could now be `foo: runtime; 142` seconds. This now allows for correct scaling on the display to *two minutes and 22 seconds*. And the user receiving an alert relating to this metric can understand that it refers to some runtime timing.

# Retrieving metrics from the server

MicroProfile Metrics exposes metrics via a REST interface, by default, under the /metrics context root. You can find the code at https://github.com/PacktPublishing/Hands-On-Enterprise-Java-Microservices-with-Eclipse-MicroProfile/tree/master/Chapter05-metrics. Follow the README.md file to build the code, run it, and hit the http://localhost:8080/book-metrics/hello and http://localhost:8080/book-metrics endpoints a few times with your browser to generate some data.

 As of MicroProfile 1.3/2.0, there is nothing in the specifications about securing that endpoint. This is thus left to the individual implementation.

Using this REST interface, it is easy to retrieve the data, for example, via the following curl command:

```
$ curl http://localhost:8080/metrics
```

This command shows the Metrics 1.x output in Prometheus text format (abbreviated):

```
# TYPE base:classloader_total_loaded_class_count counter
base:classloader_total_loaded_class_count 13752.0
# TYPE base:cpu_system_load_average gauge
base:cpu_system_load_average 2.796875
# TYPE base:thread_count counter
base:thread_count 76.0
# TYPE vendor:memory_pool_metaspace_usage_max_bytes gauge
vendor:memory_pool_metaspace_usage_max_bytes 7.0916056E7
# TYPE application:hello_time_rate_per_second gauge
application:hello_time_rate_per_second{app="shop",type="timer"}
3.169298061424996E-10
# TYPE application:hello_time_one_min_rate_per_second gauge
application:hello_time_one_min_rate_per_second{app="shop",type="timer"} 0.0
[...]
```

If you do not provide a media type, the default output format is the Prometheus text format (which can also be rendered nicely in the browser). The Prometheus format exposes additional metadata to the values in the # TYPE and # HELP lines. You can also see in the previous example how the scopes (base, vendor, and application) are prepended to the actual metrics name.

Alternatively, it is possible to retrieve data in the JSON format by providing an HAccept header (again abbreviated):

```
$ curl -HAccept:application/json http://localhost:8080/metrics
```

This command results in the following output:

```
{
 "application" :
  {
    "helloTime" : {
        "p50": 1.4884994E7,
      [...]
        "count": 1,
        "meanRate": 0.06189342578194245
      },
    "getCounted" : 1
  },
  "base" :
  {
    "classloader.totalLoadedClass.count" : 13970,
    "cpu.systemLoadAverage" : 2.572265625,
    "gc.PS Scavenge.time" : 290
  },
  "vendor" :
  {
    "test" : 271,
    "memoryPool.Metaspace.usage.max" : 72016928,
  }
```

In this case, the pure data is exposed; the scopes form a top level, and respective metrics are nested inside. Matching metadata can be retrieved via an HTTP XOPTIONS call:

```
$ curl XOPTIONS -HAccept:application/json http://localhost:8080/metrics
```

The output now contains the metadata as a map:

```
{
"application" : {
 "helloTime": {
 "unit": "nanoseconds",
 "type": "timer",
 "description": "Timing of the Hello call",
 "tags": "app=shop,type=timer",
 "displayName": "helloTime"
 }
 }
 [...]
 }
```

Now that we have seen how we can retrieve different types of data and metadata, we will have a quick look at how we can limit retrieval to specific scopes.

# Accessing specific scopes

It is also possible to retrieve data for only a single scope by appending the scope name to the path. In the following example, we only retrieve metrics for the base scope:

```
$ curl http://localhost:8080/metrics/base
```

This now only shows metrics for the base scope:

```
# TYPE base:classloader_total_loaded_class_count counter
base:classloader_total_loaded_class_count 13973.0
# TYPE base:cpu_system_load_average gauge
base:cpu_system_load_average 1.92236328125
```

In this section, we have seen how to retrieve metrics from a MicroProfile Metrics-enabled server. Metrics in base and vendor scopes are predefined by the server. Metrics in the application scope can be defined by the user, which we are going to explore in the next section.

# Supplying application-specific metrics

Applications can choose to expose metric data via a CDI programming model. This model was inspired by DropWizard Metrics, so that it is easier to transition applications to MP-Metrics. It also uses the annotations from DropWizard Metrics, which have been augmented to support metadata.

Let's start with an example by defining a counter that is then incremented in code:

```
@Inject
@Metric(absolute = true, description = "# calls to /health")
Counter hCount; // This is the counter

@GET
@Path("/health")
public Response getHealth() throws Exception {
    hCount.inc(); // It is increased in the application
    [...]
}
```

In this example, we are registering a counter by getting it injected into the hCount variable:

The @Metric annotation provides additional information, such as the description, and also indicates that the name is the variable name without an additional package (absolute=true).

In the following example, we let the implementation do the counting for us. This implements the common use case of counting the number of invocations of a method or REST endpoint:

```
@Counted(absolute=true,
         description="# calls to getCounted",
         monotonic=true)
@GET
@Path("/c")
public String getCounted() {
    return "Counted called";
}
```

The `monotonic` attribute of `@Counted` says to keep increasing the counter, otherwise it will be decreased when leaving the method.

# More types of metric

Counters are only one type of metric that can be exposed and, very often, more complex types are needed, for example, to record the distribution of the duration of method calls.

Let's have a quick look at these. Most follow the pattern of `@Counted`.

## Gauges

A gauge is a metric whose value arbitrarily goes up and down. Gauges are always backed by a method that supplies the value of the gauge:

```
@Gauge
int provideGaugeValue() {
   return 42;   // The value of the gauge is always 42
}
```

The gauge's value is computed, like all other values, when a client requests the values. This requires the implementation of the gauge method to be very quick, so that a caller is not blocked.

## Meter

A meter measures the rate at which the decorated method is called over time. For a JAX-RS endpoint, this would be the number of requests per second. Meters can be declared via an annotation:

```
@GET
@Path("/m")
@Metered(absolute = true)
public String getMetered() {
  return "Metered called";
}
```

When a client requests the data from the meter, the server supplies the mean rate, as well as one-, five-, and fifteen-minute moving averages. The latter may be familiar to some readers from the Unix/Linux `uptime` command.

## Histograms

A histogram is a type of metric that samples the distribution of data. It is mostly used to record the distribution of the time it takes to execute the decorated method. Histograms cannot be declared via dedicated annotation, unlike other types, but a timer, for example, includes histogram data. To use a histogram on its own, you need to register and update it in code:

```
// Register the Histogram
@Inject
@Metric(absolute = true)
private Histogram aHistogram;

// Update with a value from 0 to 10
@GET
@Path("/h")
public String getHistogram() {
  aHistogram.update((int) (Math.random() * 10.0));
  return "Histogram called";
}
```

This way of using metrics in code is feasible for the other types as well.

## Timers

A timer basically is a combination of a histogram and a meter and can again be declared via an annotation:

```
@GET
@Path("/hello")
@Timed(name="helloTime", absolute = true,
        description = "Timing of the Hello call",
        tags={"type=timer","app=shop"})
public String getHelloTimed() {
  try {
    Thread.sleep((long) (Math.random()*200.0));
  } catch (InterruptedException e) {
      // We don't care if the sleep is interrupted.
  }
  return "Hello World";
}
```

The code in this example waits for a small random amount of time to make the output a bit more interesting.

# Tagging

Tags or labels are a way to additionally organize information. These became popular with Docker and Kubernetes. Within MicroProfile Metrics 1.x, they are directly forwarded to the output without further ado and do not serve to distinguish metrics. MicroProfile Metrics supports server-wide and per-metrics tags, which are then merged together in the output.

## Server-wide tags

Server-wide tags are set via the environment variable, MP_METRICS_TAGS, as shown:

```
export MP_METRICS_TAGS=app=myShop
java -jar target/metrics-thorntail.jar
```

These tags will be added to all metrics defined in the server and also added to the respective output format.

So, given the preceding command, a counter, @Counted(absolute=true) int myCount;, would end up in Prometheus as follows:

```
# TYPE application:my_count counter
application:my_count{app="myShop"} 0
```

### Per-metrics tags

Tags can also be supplied on a per-metric basis:

```
@Counted(tags=["version=v1","commit=abcde"])
void doSomething() {
  [...]
}
```

This example defines two labels, `version=v1` and `commit=abcde`, on the metric with the name `doSomething`. Those will be merged with the global tags for the output. With the preceding global tag, there would thus be three tags in the output.

In this section, we have seen how to add labels to metrics to provide additional metadata. These can be global, for all metrics exposed from a server, or application-specific, for one single metric.

# Using Prometheus to retrieve metrics

Now that we have seen what metrics are exposed and how we can define our own, let's have a look at how we can collect them in a **time series database (TSDB)**. For this purpose, we use Prometheus, a CNCF (`https://www.cncf.io/`) project that has gained widespread adoption in the cloud-native world.

You can download Prometheus from `https://prometheus.io` or on macOS via `brew install prometheus`.

Once Prometheus is downloaded, we need a configuration file that defines which targets to scrape and can then start the server. For our purposes, we will use the following simple file:

```
.Prometheus configuration for a Thorntail Server, prom.yml
scrape_configs:
# Configuration to poll from Thorntail
- job_name: 'thorntail'
  scrape_interval: 15s
  # translates to http://localhost:8080/metrics
  static_configs:
    - targets: ['localhost:8080']
```

 The configuration for Prometheus is different for different servers, as MicroProfile Metrics only specifies the content of the endpoint, but not its location. OpenLiberty, for example, uses a password and TLS-protected endpoint on port 9443.

With that, we can start Prometheus via `prometheus --config.file prom.yml`.

Give it a moment and then head over to the Prometheus web console at `http://localhost:9090` and then to the `http://localhost:9090/targets`[*Status->Targets*] entry.

You will see our server being detected:

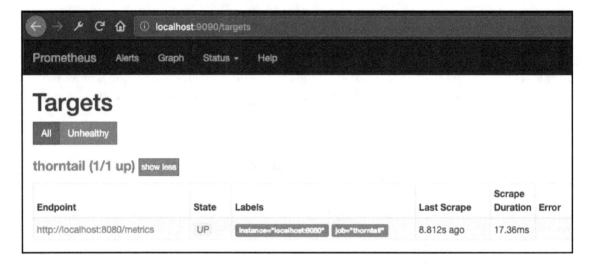

When everything is OK, you can click on **Prometheus** in the top-left corner or select the **Graph** menu. You are presented with a text field. Start entering *base* and you'll see a list of metrics. Selecting one of them and then clicking on the **Graph** tab yields a simple but nice graph of the metric:

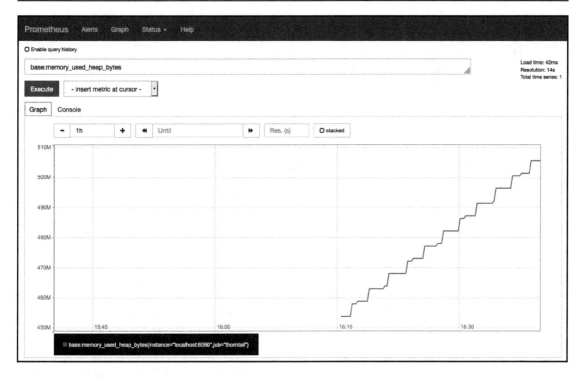

Application metrics will not show up directly after the start, as they may only be created programmatically when the code that creates them is executed for the first time.

A good practice though is to initialize metrics close to the start of the application if possible.

# New in MP-Metrics 2.0

NOTE: MicroProfile Metrics 2.0 may not be released when you read this, and the content may have changed slightly depending on feedback from early users/implementors.

# Change for counters – introducing ConcurrentGauge

Counters in Metrics 1.x had two functions:

- To provide a measure for the number of concurrent invocations
- As a metric that can count up to the number of transactions committed, for example

Unfortunately, the first way was the default when using the annotation without specifying the `monotonic` keyword, which is unexpected and was confusing a lot of users. The second version of this also had its issues, as a counter value could also decrease at will, which violates the understanding that a counter is a monotonically increasing metric.

For this reason, the Metrics working group has decided to change the behavior of counters so they only work as monotonically increasing metrics and to defer the use case of counting concurrent invocations to a new metric type, the ConcurrentGauge. As with most other metrics, ConcurrentGauge can be used as a type or by annotating a method.

# Tagging

Tags now also serve to distinguish metrics with the same name and type, but different tags. They could be used to support many metrics `result_code` on a REST endpoint to count the number of (un)successful calls:

```
@Inject
@Metric(tags="{code,200}", name="result_code")
Counter result_code_200k;

@Inject
@Metric(tags="{code,500}", name="result_code")
Counter result_code_500;

@GET
@Path("/")
public String getData(String someParam) {

  String result = getSomeData(someParam);
  if (result == null ) {
    result_code_500.inc();
  } else {
    result_code_200.inc();
  }
  return result;
}
```

Under the covers, metrics are no longer only keyed by name and type, but also by their tags. For this, new `MetricID` has been introduced to host the name and the tags.

## Changes in data output format

The introduction of multi-tag metrics in MicroProfile Metrics 2.0 necessitated changes in the format of metric data that is made available to clients.

The Prometheus format also had some inconsistencies, so we decided to revamp the formats in sometimes incompatible ways:

- The colon (:) as a separator between the scope and metric name has been changed to an underscore (_).
- The Prometheus output format no longer requires that camelCase is turned into snake_case.
- The format of the base metrics for garbage collectors has changed and now uses tags for the various garbage collectors.

Please consult the release notes in the MicroProfile 2.0 specification at `https://github.com/eclipse/microprofile-metrics/releases/tag/2.0` for more details.

MicroProfile Metrics facilitates the gathering of performance data from individual servers over an HTTP-based API for alerting and capacity planning purposes. In a microservice architecture, this is not enough to troubleshoot, for example, latency issues that an end user may be seeing. OpenTracing can help here in finding the service that is causing the slowdown. Looking at the telemetry of the service can then help to pin down the issue further.

Now, let's discuss OpenTracing.

# MicroProfile OpenTracing

In the modern world of microservices, a single request can traverse multiple processes running on different machines, data centers, or even geographical regions.

The observability of such systems is a challenging task but, when done right, it allows us to *tell the story* about each individual request as opposed to the overall state of the system derived from signals such as metrics and logs. In this chapter, we will introduce you to distributed tracing and explain OpenTracing with its integration in MicroProfile OpenTracing 1.3.

In the previous section, we learned about metrics and how they observe an application or each individual component. This information is no doubt very valuable and provides a macro view of the system, but, at the same time, it says very little about each individual request that traverses multiple components. Distributed tracing shows a micro view of what happened with a request end to end so that we can retrospectively understand the behavior of each individual component of the application.

Distributed tracing is action-based; in other words, it records everything related to an action in the system. For example, it captures detailed information of a request and all causally related activities. We will not go through the details of how this tracing works, but, in a nutshell, we can state the following:

- The tracing infrastructure attaches contextual metadata to each request, typically, a set of unique IDs – `traceId`, `spanId`, and `parentId`.
- The instrumentation layer records profiling data and propagates metadata inside and between processes.
- The captured profiling data contains metadata and causality references to preceding events.

Based on the captured data, distributed tracing systems usually offer the following functionality:

- Root-cause analysis
- Latency optimization – critical path analysis
- Distributed context propagation – baggage
- Contextualized logging
- Service dependency analysis

Before we delve into MicroProfile OpenTracing, let's briefly look at OpenTracing so that we can better understand what the API offers.

# OpenTracing project

The OpenTracing project (`https://opentracing.io`) provides a vendor-neutral specification (`https://github.com/opentracing/specification`) and polyglot APIs for describing distributed transactions. Vendor neutrality is important because code instrumentation is the most time-consuming and challenging task when enabling distributed tracing in large organizations. We would like to stress that OpenTracing is just an API. A real deployment will require a plugged tracer implementation that runs inside the monitored process and sends data to a tracing system.

From an API perspective, there are three key concepts: Tracer, Span, and SpanContext. Tracer is a singleton object available to the application that can be used to model a unit of work by creating a Span instance. A Span typically models an invocation in the system – a request or a method call. A set of spans (directed acyclic graph) is called a trace and represents end-to-end invocation. This object is not directly represented in API and it is modeled as a list of Spans. Spans hold timing information, tags, and logs. Context metadata and causality information are encapsulated in an object called SpanContext.

The following diagram demonstrates tracing for two services:

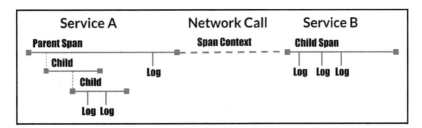

Let's now discuss the configuration part.

# Configuration properties

OpenTracing is vendor-neutral and can, therefore, work with any vendor's tracing implementation that uses this API. Each tracer implementation will be configured differently. Therefore, the configuration is outside the scope of the MicroProfile OpenTracing specification. However, the specification itself exposes a couple of configuration properties to adjust the tracing scope or generated data. The configuration leverages the MicroProfile Config specification to provide a consistent means for all supported configuration options.

Currently, the specification exposes the following:

- `mp.opentracing.server.skip-pattern`: A skip pattern to avoid the tracing of selected REST endpoints.
- `mp.opentracing.server.operation-name-provider`: This specifies the operation name provider for server spans. Possible values are `http-path` and `class-method`. The default value is `class-method`, which fully uses a qualified class name concatenated with a method name; for example, `GET:org.eclipse.Service.get`. The `http-path` uses a value of `@Path` annotation as an operation name.

# Automatic instrumentation

The motivation here is to have tracing automatically capture all crucial performance information and also automatically propagate tracing context between runtimes. The second part is especially crucial because it ensures that traces are not broken and we are able to investigate end-to-end invocation. For successful tracing, every communication technology between runtimes has to be instrumented. In the case of MicroProfile, it is JAX-RS and MicroProfile Rest Client.

## JAX-RS

MicroProfile OpenTracing automatically traces all inbound JAX-RS endpoints. However, the JAX-RS client side is more tricky and requires the registration API, `org.eclipse.microprofile.opentracing.ClientTracingRegistrar.configure(ClientBuilder clientBuilder)`, to be called to add tracing capability. MicroProfile implementation can enable tracing for all client interfaces globally; however, it is recommended to use the registration API for better portability.

The default tracing behavior can be modified by disabling the tracing of specific requests or changing operation names of produced server spans. For more information, refer to the *Configuration properties* section later in this chapter. The instrumentation layer automatically adds the following request-scoped information to each span:

- `http.method`: The HTTP method of the request.
- `http.status_code`: The status code of the request.
- `http.url`: The URL of the request.
- `component`: The name of the instrumented component, `jaxrs`.
- `span.kind`: The client or server.
- `error` – `true` or `false`. This is optional and, if present, instrumentation also adds an exception as `error.object` to span logs.

All these tags can be used to query data via the tracing system user interface, or they can be used for data analytics jobs that many tracing systems provide. Additional metadata can be added to the current active span via an injected tracer instance. This can be conducted globally in filters or locally in rest handlers, as shown in the following code example, by adding a user agent header to the server span (1):

```
@Path("/")
public class JaxRsService {
    @Inject
    private io.opentracing.Tracer tracer;
```

```
@GET
@Path("/hello")
@Traced(operationName="greeting") (2)
public String hello(@HeaderParam("user-agent") String userAgent) {
    tracer.activeSpan().setTag("user-agent", userAgent); (1)
}
}
```

By default, server-side spans have the operation name
`http_method:package.className.method`. However, this can be changed locally by
using the `@Traced` annotation (2), or globally via the configuration property (refer to the
configuration section).

## MicroProfile Rest Client

As was mentioned in the previous section, all REST client interfaces are, by default,
automatically traced with no additional configuration required. This behavior can be
changed by applying the `@Traced` annotation to the interface or method to disable tracing.
When applied to the interface, all methods are skipped from tracing. Note that the tracing
context is not being propagated. Therefore, if the request continues to an instrumented
runtime, a new trace is started.

## Explicit instrumentation

Sometimes, the automatic instrumentation does not capture all critical timing information
and, therefore, additional trace points are needed. For example, we would like to trace an
invocation of a business layer or initialize third-party instrumentation provided by the
OpenTracing project (`https://github.com/opentracing-contrib`).

The explicit instrumentation can be done in three ways:

- Add the `@Traced` annotation on **Context and Dependency Injection (CDI)**
  beans.
- Inject the tracer and create spans manually.
- Initialize third-party instrumentation. The initialization of external
  instrumentation depends on its own initialization requirements. MicroProfile just
  has to provide a tracer instance, which is covered in the previous bullet point.

Let's now discuss these in detail.

# @Traced annotation

MicroProfile OpenTracing defines an `@Traced` annotation that can be used to enable tracing on CDI beans or disable tracing on automatically traced interfaces. The annotation can also be used to override the operation name on other automatically traced components – JAX-RS endpoints.

The following code example shows how the `@Traced` annotation can be used to enable tracing on a CDI bean. (1) enables tracing for all methods the bean defines. (2) overrides the default operation name (`package.className.method`) to `get_all_users`. (3) disables tracing of the health method:

```
@Traced (1)
@ApplicationScoped
public class Service {
    @Traced(operationName = "get_all_users") (2)
    public void getUsers() {
        // business code
    }

    @Traced(false) (3)
    public void health() {
        // business code
    }
}
```

Now, we will look at the next method.

# Tracer injection

The application can inject an `io.opentracing.Tracer` bean that exposes the full OpenTracing API. This allows application developers to leverage more advanced use cases, such as adding metadata to the currently active span, manually creating spans, using baggage for context propagation, or initializing additional third-party instrumentation.

The following code shows how the tracer is used to attach data to the currently active span, (1):

```
@Path("/")
public class Service {
    @Inject
    private Tracer tracer;

    @GET
    @Path("")
    @Produces(MediaType.TEXT_PLAIN)
    public String greeting() {
        tracer.activeSpan()
            .setTag("greeting", "hello"); (1)
        return "hello";
    }
}
```

This can be useful for adding business-related data to spans, but also to log exceptions or any other profiling information.

# Tracing with Jaeger

So far, we have only talked about different aspects of the instrumentation. However, to run the full tracing infrastructure, we need a tracing backend. In this section, we will use Jaeger (`https://www.jaegertracing.io/`) to demonstrate how collected tracing data is presented in a tracing system. We have chosen Jaeger because Thorntail provides direct integration with Jaeger. Other vendors can provide integrations with other systems, for instance, Zipkin, and Instana. Almost every tracing system offers a Gannt chart style view (or timeline) of a trace. This view might be overwhelming for tracing novices, but it is a great tool to systematically analyze an invocation in a distributed system.

The following screenshot shows a search screen in the Jaeger system. In this case, we are searching for traces from the `opentracing-example` service and all operations.

The example application, with instructions on how to run it, can be found in the attached Git repository:

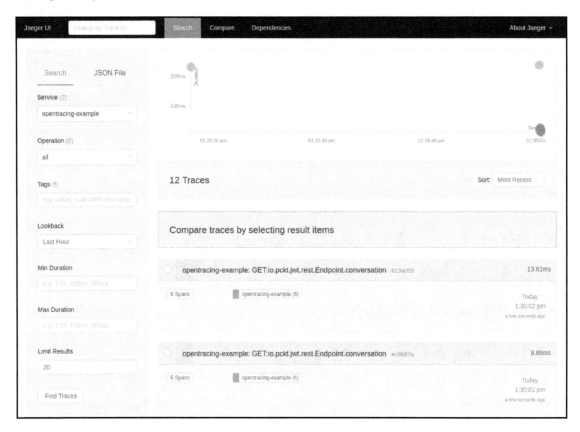

The following screenshot shows a timeline view (end-to-end invocation) of a chaining REST invocation from /conversation to /bonjour within the same service. The source code can be found in the attached Git repository:

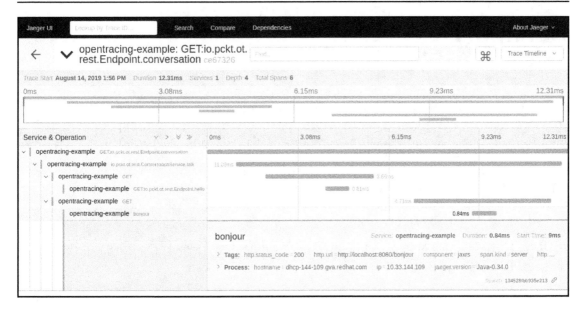

Each horizontal line represents one unit of work or invocation a (span in OpenTracing terminology).

On the left-hand side, there are service names (*opentracing-example*) with operation names. The first operation is GET:io.pckt.ot.rest.Endpoint.conversaion for the server-side endpoint, /conversation. The right-hand side shows duration relative to other invocations (blue lines). From this view, it is obvious that the first operation was the longest (12.31 ms) and it was blocked until all descendant operations finished. The bottom part of the screen shows an expanded view of the last span (the *bonjour* operation) where we can see all metadata attached to the span.

# Summary

In this chapter, we learned about the observability of servers and applications.

Metrics, or telemetry, can help to pinpoint the performance characteristics of a server or an application. MicroProfile offers, via the Metrics specification, a way to export Metrics in standardized ways. Application writers can use MicroProfile Metrics to expose their data to monitoring clients decoratively via annotations or via calls to the Metrics API.

The chapter further explained how OpenTracing integration in MicroProfile provides an end-to-end view for each individual transaction going through the system. We went through the configuration properties, showcasing tracing for JAX-RS, and finally investigating data in the Jaeger system.

In the next chapter, we will learn how to document (REST) APIs via OpenAPI and call those APIs via the type-safe REST client.

# Questions

1. What is the difference between distributed tracing and metrics?
2. What functionality do distributed tracing systems usually provide?
3. What parts of the system are automatically traced in MicroProfile OpenTracing?
4. Which tags are added for every REST request by MicroProfile OpenTracing?
5. How can explicit instrumentation be added to the business code?
6. What are scopes in Metrics and what is their rationale?
7. What determines the output format of a REST request to the Metrics API?
8. What ways are available to export metrics within a user application?

# 6
# MicroProfile OpenAPI and Type-Safe REST Client

Eclipse MicroProfile has a rich set of specifications for Java microservices. Two of these, Eclipse MicroProfile OpenAPI and Eclipse MicroProfile REST Client, help with the API documentation for your microservices and provide an API for type-safe invocation on REST endpoints, respectively. OpenAPI simplifies the documentation for microservice endpoints and makes this metadata available for perusal by third-party developers. A type-safe REST client simplifies the marshalling and unmarshalling of objects to HTTP or JSON.

The following topics will be covered in this chapter:

- The capabilities offered by each of these specifications
- Simple code examples of some of these capabilities
- How to obtain further information about each of these specifications

## Introduction to MicroProfile OpenAPI and its capabilities

The mobile force that fuels the digital economy led to the need for businesses to establish an omni-channel approach to development in order to optimize costs, increase efficiencies, and improve customer experience. A facilitator of this approach was APIs, which led to the API economy and concepts such as API-led or API-first development practices. In addition, the microservices architecture has become the architecture of choice for modern development. API-based (that is, RESTful) communication among microservices has been adopted as the *de facto* standard because it is a good fit for the *smart endpoints and dumb pipes*, *decentralized governance*, and *decentralized data management* characteristics of microservices.

However, as the number of microservices increases in a microservices architecture, their management can become unwieldy. However, you can manage your microservices via their APIs. You can apply management, security, load balancing, and throttling policies to the APIs that are fronting your microservices.

Eclipse MicroProfile OpenAPI provides Java interfaces to developers for generating OpenAPI v3 documents from their Java RESTful Web Services (JAX-RS) applications. The specification requires that a fully processed OpenAPI document be available at the root URL, /openapi, as an HTTP GET operation, as follows:

```
GET http://myHost:myPort/openapi
```

The required protocol is http. However, implementors of the specification are strongly encouraged to also support the https protocol for secure connectivity to the OpenAPI endpoint.

There are three sources from which the OpenAPI document is created. These three sources (described in later sections in this chapter) are as follows:

- Generated by processing the JAX-RS annotations (and optional OpenAPI annotations) found in the application
- Programmatically built by an application by providing a Java class that implements OasModelReader
- A static OpenAPI document included in application deployment

These three sources (any combination) are combined to produce a single OpenAPI document, which can be filtered (by providing a Java class that implements the OasFilter interface) and then served at the preceding /openapi endpoint.

# Configuration

The MicroProfile OpenAPI specification makes use of the MicroProfile configuration specification to configure its parameters and values. For example, for injecting configuration values, MicroProfile OpenAPI can use the default and custom ConfigSources.

 For more information on ConfigSources, you can visit https://github. com/eclipse/microprofile-config/blob/master/spec/src/main/ asciidoc/configsources.asciidoc.

There are many configurable items. The following table contains a subset of them:

| Configuration item | Description |
|---|---|
| `mp.openapi.scan.disable` | Configuration property to disable annotation scanning. The default value is `false`. |
| `mp.openapi.servers` | Configuration property to specify the list of global servers that provide connectivity information; for example, `mp.openapi.servers=https://xyz.com/v1,https://abc.com/v1.` |
| `mp.openapi.servers.path` | Prefix of the configuration property to specify an alternative list of servers to service all operations in a path; for example, `mp.openapi.servers.path./airlines/bookings/{id}=https://xyz.io/v1.` |
| `mp.openapi.servers.operation` | Prefix of the configuration property to specify an alternative list of servers to service an operation. Operations that want to specify an alternative list of servers must define an `operationId`, a unique string used to identify the operation; for example, `mp.openapi.servers.operation.getBooking=https://abc.io/v1.` |

For a complete list of configuration items, please refer to the Eclipse MicroProfile OpenAPI specification document at the following location – `https://github.com/eclipse/microprofile-open-api`, which is also listed at the end of the chapter.

# Generating the OpenAPI document

As already described, the MicroProfile OpenAPI specification requires that an OpenAPI document be generated from a combination of three sources.

You then have a number of choices:

- Extend the OpenAPI document generated by the JAX-RS annotations using the MicroProfile OpenAPI annotations.
- Leverage the initial output from `/openapi`, which you can use as a reference to start documenting your APIs. In this case, you can write static OpenAPI files (described in a later section in this chapter) before any code is written, which is a usual approach adopted by organizations to lock-in the contract of the API, that is, it is an API-first development practice.
- Bootstrap or complete the OpenAPI model tree by coding using the programming model, covered later in this chapter.

Additionally, you can use a filter to update the OpenAPI model after it has been built.

# MicroProfile OpenAPI annotations

Probably the most common source of OpenAPI information is the set of annotations that make up the definition of a standard JAX-RS application. These annotations, along with additional (optional) annotations defined by the MicroProfile OpenAPI specification, can be scanned and processed by the MicroProfile platform to produce an OpenAPI document.

The MP OpenAPI specification requires the generation of a valid OpenAPI document from pure JAX-RS 2.0 applications. If you are new to OpenAPI, you can simply deploy your existing JAX-RS application to a MicroProfile OpenAPI runtime and check out the output from /openapi.

To fill out additional details of the generated OpenAPI document, you may further annotate your JAX-RS application with the many annotations defined by the MicroProfile OpenAPI specification. The following table contains a partial list of these additional annotations:

| Annotation | Description |
|---|---|
| @APIResponse | Describes a single response from an API operation |
| @Content | Provides a schema and examples for a particular media type |
| @Operation | Describes an operation or typically a HTTP method against a specific path |
| @Parameter | Describes a single parameter of an operation |
| @Schema | Allows the definition of input and output data types |

For a complete list of annotations, please refer to the MicroProfile OpenAPI specification document listed at the end of this chapter.

# Usage examples

Some usage examples of MicroProfile OpenAPI annotations are as follows:

Example 1 – Simple operation description (abbreviated):

```
@GET
@Path("/findByMake")
@Operation(summary = "Finds cars by make",
           description = "Find cars by their manufacturer")
public Response findCarsByMake(...)
{ ... }
```

The following is the output for example 1:

```
/car/findByMake:
  get:
    summary: Finds cars by make
    description: Find cars by their manufacturer
```

Example 2 – Operation with different responses (abbreviated):

```
@GET
@Path("/{name}")
@Operation(summary = "Get customer by name")
  @APIResponse(description = "The customer",
            content = @Content(mediaType = "application/json",
                            schema = @Schema(implementation =
Customer.class))),
@APIResponse(responseCode = "400", description = "Customer not found")
public Response getCustomerByName(
        @Parameter(description = "The name of the customer to be fetched",
required = true) @PathParam("name") String name)

{...}
```

The following is the output for example 2:

```
/customer/{name}:
    get:
        summary: Get customer by name
        operationId: getCutomerByName
        parameters:
        - name: name
          in: path
          description: 'The name of the customer to be fetched'
          required: true
          schema:
            type: string
        responses:
          default:
            description: The customer
            content:
              application/json:
                schema:
                  $ref: '#/components/schemas/Customer'
          400:
            description: Customer not found
```

For more examples, please refer to the MicroProfile OpenAPI specification wiki at `https://github.com/eclipse/microprofile-open-api/wiki`.

# Static OpenAPI files

As mentioned earlier in the chapter, static OpenAPI files are one of the three sources from which the OpenAPI document can be created. In the following, we give you a short introductory description of how you could generate one and how to include it in your deployment. Many organizations use an API-first development practice, which entails defining static OpenAPI files even before any code is implemented for them.

First, you can create an OpenAPI document by using an open source editor such as Swagger Editor (`https://editor.swagger.io`). The following is a screenshot shows this:

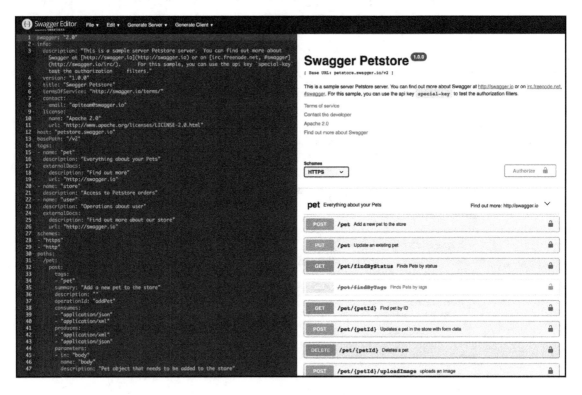

Using this editor, you can start with sample API definitions and modify them to your needs or you can start typing afresh. Ensure that the document is converted to OpenAPI 3 by selecting **Convert to OpenAPI 3** in the **Edit** menu as follows:

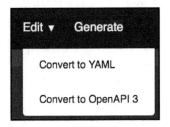

When you are finished defining your APIs in the document, export them as YAML by selecting **Save as YAML** in the **File** menu as follows:

Finally, you can include the saved OpenAPI document in your application deployment.

 If a document is fully complete, then set the `mp.openapi.scan.disable` configuration property to `true`. If a document is partially complete, then you will need to augment the OpenAPI snippet with annotations or the programming model.

Vendors are required to fetch a single document named `openapi` with an extension of `.yml`, `.yaml`, or `json` inside the application module's (that is, the WAR artifact's) `META-INF` folder.

# Programming model

You can provide OpenAPI elements via Java POJOs (Plain Old Java Objects) by using the MicroProfile OpenAPI programming model. The complete set of models is described in the `org.eclipse.microprofile.openapi.models` package. You can read more about it at `https://github.com/eclipse/microprofile-open-api/tree/master/api/src/main/java/org/eclipse/microprofile/openapi/models`.

You can create an OpenAPI tree by using `OASFactory`. Refer to the following code block by way of an example:

```
OASFactory.createObject(Info.class).title("Weather")
          .description("Weather APIs").version("1.0.0");
```

To bootstrap the OpenAPI model tree, you can use the `OASModelReader` interface. You can then create an implementation of this interface and register it using the `mp.openapi.model.reader` configuration key.

The following is globally an example of what its definition would look like in `META-INF/microprofile-config.properties`:

```
mp.openapi.model.reader=com.mypackage.MyModelReader
```

> Like static files, the model reader can be used to provide either complete or partial model trees. To provide a complete OpenAPI model tree, you should set the `mp.openapi.scan.disable` configuration to `true`. Otherwise, this partial model will be assumed.

# Using a filter for updates

To update or remove certain elements and fields of the OpenAPI document, you can use a filter. The OASFilter (`https://github.com/eclipse/microprofile-open-api/blob/master/api/src/main/java/org/eclipse/microprofile/openapi/OASFilter.java`) interface allows you to receive callbacks for various OpenAPI elements. It allows you to override the methods you care about. You can create an implementation of this interface and register it using the `mp.openapi.filter` configuration key.

Here's an example of what its definition would look like in `META-INF/microprofile-config.properties`:

```
mp.openapi.filter=com.mypackage.MyFilter
```

A registered filter is called once for each model element. For example, the `filterPathItem` method is called for each corresponding `PathItem` element in the model tree.

 The MicroProfile OpenAPI project can be found at the following link: `https://github.com/eclipse/microprofile-open-api`.

MicroProfile OpenAPI enables the generation of API documentation for your microservices. For organizations using an API-first development approach, MicroProfile OpenAPI helps them to define their APIs before any coding is done for their corresponding microservices. In addition, for organizations that may already have REST-based microservices, MicroProfile OpenAPI can automatically generate API documentation. In the next section, we delve into how you can leverage the capabilities of the MicroProfile REST Client to create endpoints for your microservices.

# Introduction to the MicroProfile REST Client and its capabilities

The **MicroProfile REST Client** (**MP-RC**) provides an API for type-safe invocation on REST endpoints. It can be used from applications to perform remote invocations on other services.

It leverages JAX-RS annotations on Java interfaces to describe the actual contract with remotes services. These interfaces are then used to create client proxies that hide much of the underlying HTTP communication.

The MP-RC specification defines the requirements for leveraging the JAX-RS annotations on the Java interface, as well as MP-RC-specific annotations to augment behavior, including how incoming request headers should be propagated, how to augment JAX-RS behaviors using providers, exception mapping, CDI support, and integration with other MicroProfile specifications. We will look at MP-RC in more detail by starting with the definition of a type-safe endpoint interface.

# Defining the endpoint Interface

To define the type-safe interface for an endpoint, we create a Java interface that leverages JAX-RS annotations to map interface methods to the REST endpoint they proxy. A basic example is illustrated in the following `WorldClockApi` interface:

```java
package io.pckt.restc.contract;

import javax.ws.rs.GET;
import javax.ws.rs.Path;
import javax.ws.rs.PathParam;
import javax.ws.rs.Produces;
import javax.ws.rs.core.MediaType;

@Path("/api/json")
public interface WorldClockApi {
  static final String BASE_URL = "http://worldclockapi.com/api/json";

 @GET
 @Path("/utc/now")
 @Produces(MediaType.APPLICATION_JSON)
 Now utc();

 @GET
 @Path("{tz}/now")
 @Produces(MediaType.APPLICATION_JSON)
 Now tz(@PathParam("tz") String tz);
 }
public class Now {
  String currentDateTime;
  String utcOffset;
  boolean isDayLightSavingsTime;
  String dayOfTheWeek;
  String timeZoneName;
 ...
 // Getter/Setter
 }
```

Here, two interface methods are defined, `utc()` and `tz()`. Both represent GET HTTP method type requests, and both return `application/json` content types in the form of a **Plain Old Java Object (POJO)** bean. The `utc()` method accepts no parameters and has an endpoint path of `/api/json/utc/now`. The `tz()` method accepts a `tz` parameter taken from the request path using the JAX-RS `@PathParam` annotation, and has an endpoint path of `/api/json/{tz}/now`, where the `{tz}` reference corresponds to the 3-letter time zone name that is used in the request, for example, `/api/json/cst/now` for central standard time in the US.

All built-in HTTP methods are supported by the client API. Likewise, all the following parameter types are supported:

- `javax.ws.rs.QueryParam`
- `javax.ws.rs.BeanParam`
- `javax.ws.rs.CookieParam`
- `javax.ws.rs.PathParam`
- `javax.ws.rs.FormParam`
- `javax.ws.rs.MatrixParam`

If you are only interested in the body of a request response, you can return a POJO, as was done previously. Otherwise, you can return a `javax.ws.rs.Response` object and parse the body and header information from the server response.

Users may specify the media (MIME) type of the outbound request using the JAX-RS `@Consumes` annotation, which would be passed as the content-type HTTP header in the request, and the expected media type(s) of the response by using the JAX-RS `@Produces` annotation, which would be passed as the accept HTTP header. If no `@Consumes` or `@Produces` annotation is specified for a given interface method, it will default to `javax.ws.rs.core.MediaType.APPLICATION_JSON`, or `application/json`.

# MicroProfile REST Client programmatic API usage

MP-RC supports both programmatic lookup and CDI injection approaches for usage. An example of a REST service making use of `org.eclipse.microprofile.rest.client.RestClientBuilder` to create a type-safe client for the `WorldClockApi` interface is listed in the following as `WorldClockUser.java`:

```
package io.pckt.restc.contract;

import javax.ws.rs.GET;
import javax.ws.rs.Path;
import javax.ws.rs.PathParam;
import javax.ws.rs.Produces;
import javax.ws.rs.core.MediaType;

@Path("/api")
@ApplicationScoped
```

```
public class WorldClockUser {
 @GET
 @Path("/now-utc")
 @Produces(MediaType.TEXT_PLAIN)
 public String getCurrentDateTime() {
 WorldClockApi remoteApi = RestClientBuilder.newBuilder()
 .baseUri(URI.create(WorldClockApi.BASE_URL))
 .build(WorldClockApi.class);
 Now now = remoteApi.utc();
 return now.getCurrentDateTime();
 }
}
```

The `baseUri()` method is used to specify the server URI against which the `WorldClockApi` method paths are to be resolved. The `build()` method takes the Java interface of the type-safe client that is to be built. Additional `RestClientBuilder` methods include the following:

- `baseUrl(URL)`: Similar to `baseUri`, but takes a `java.net.URL` type.
- `connectTimeout(long timeout, TimeUnit unit)`: The amount of time to wait to connect to the remote server. A value of 0 indicates having to wait forever.
- `readTimeout(long timeout, TimeUnit unit)`: The amount of time to wait on reads of the remote server connection. A value of 0 indicates having to wait forever.
- `executorService(ExecutorService executor)`: Used for async requests. We will return to this in the async section.

# MicroProfile REST Client CDI usage

MP-RC type-safe interfaces may be injected as CDI beans. The runtime must create a CDI bean for each interface annotated with `@RegisterRestClient`. A CDI client injects bean created will include a qualifier, `@RestClient`, to differentiate use as an MP-RC injection point. The following update to our `WorldClockApi` interface illustrates the use of the `@RegisterRestClient` annotation:

```
import javax.ws.rs.GET;
import javax.ws.rs.Path;
import javax.ws.rs.PathParam;
import javax.ws.rs.Produces;
import javax.ws.rs.core.MediaType;

import org.eclipse.microprofile.rest.client.inject.RegisterRestClient;
```

```
@Path("/api/json")
@RegisterRestClient()
public interface WorldClockApi {
 static final String BASE_URL = "http://worldclockapi.com/api/json";
 ...
}
```

An alternative client that makes use of CDI to obtain a `WorldClockApi` MP-RC interface is shown in the following `WorldClockCDIUser.java` snippet:

```
import org.eclipse.microprofile.rest.client.inject.RestClient;
@ApplicationScoped
@Path("/cdi")
public class WorldClockCDIUser {
 @Inject
 @RestClient
 WorldClockApi remoteApi;

 @GET
 @Path("/now-utc")
 @Produces(MediaType.TEXT_PLAIN)
 public String getCurrentDateTime() {
 Now now = remoteApi.utc();
 return now.getCurrentDateTime();
 }
}
```

The client injects the `WorldClockApi` interface, and the MP-RC implementation is responsible for producing the type-safe proxy to be injected.

## MicroProfile Config integration

For CDI-defined interfaces, it is possible to use MicroProfile Config properties to define additional behaviors that are available via the `RestClientBuilder` API. Given our `io.pckt.restc.contract.WorldClockApi` interface, the following MicroProfile Config properties are available to control the generated proxy behavior:

- `io.pckt.restc.contract.WorldClockApi/mp-rest/url`: The base URL to use for this service, the equivalent of the `RestClientBuilder#baseUrl` method.
- `io.pckt.restc.contract.WorldClockApi/mp-rest/scope`: The fully qualified class name to a CDI scope to use for injection; it defaults to `javax.enterprise.context.Dependent`.

- `io.pckt.restc.contract.WorldClockApi/mp-rest/providers`: A comma-separated list of fully qualified provider class names to include in the client, the equivalent of the `RestClientBuilder#register` method or the `@RegisterProvider` annotation.
- `io.pckt.restc.contract.WorldClockApi/mp-rest/providers/com.mycompany.MyProvider/priority`: This will override the priority of the `com.mycompany.MyProvider` provider for this interface.
- `io.pckt.restc.contract.WorldClockApi/mp-rest/connectTimeout`: The timeout specified in milliseconds to wait to connect to the remote endpoint.
- `io.pckt.restc.contract.WorldClockApi/mp-rest/readTimeout`: The timeout specified in milliseconds to wait for a response from the remote endpoint.

## Simplifying configuration keys

Since the default MP Config property names for a CDI interface can be quite long due to the inclusion of the interface package name, the MP-RC specification supports a way to simplify the property name prefix using the `configKey` attribute of the `@RegisterRestClient` annotation:

```
@Path("/api/json")
@RegisterRestClient(baseUri = WorldClockApi.BASE_URL, configKey =
"worldClock")
public interface WorldClockApi {
 static final String BASE_URL = "http://worldclockapi.com/api/json";
 ...
}
```

With the `worldClock` configKey, the previous list of property names simplifies to the following:

- `worldClock/mp-rest/url`
- `worldClock/mp-rest/uri`
- `worldClock/mp-rest/scope`
- `worldClock/mp-rest/providers`
- `worldClock/mp-rest/providers/com.mycompany.MyProvider/priority`
- `worldClock/mp-rest/connectTimeout`
- `worldClock/mp-rest/readTimeout`

The same configKey value can be used with more than one interface, and this would allow more than one interface to be configured with a single MP Config property.

# Dealing with client headers

Let's say you want to specify credentials in the HTTP authorization header to a secure remote service, but you do not want to have a string authHeader parameter in the client interface method. The MP-RC @ClientHeaderParam annotation can be used to specify HTTP headers that should be sent without altering the client interface method signature.

The following example illustrates two uses of the @ClientHeaderParam annotation to provide a User-Agent HTTP header in a variation of the WorldClockApi interface:

```java
WorldClockApiWithHeaders.java
public interface WorldClockApiWithHeaders {
 static final String BASE_URL = "http://worldclockapi.com/api/json";

 default String lookupUserAgent() {
 Config config = ConfigProvider.getConfig();
 String userAgent = config.getValue("WorldClockApi.userAgent",
String.class);
 if(userAgent == null) {
 userAgent = "MicroProfile REST Client 1.2";
 }
 return userAgent;
 }

 @GET
 @Path("/utc/now")
 @Produces(MediaType.APPLICATION_JSON)
 @ClientHeaderParam(name = "User-Agent", value = "{lookupUserAgent}")
 Now utc();

 @GET
 @Path("{tz}/now")
 @Produces(MediaType.APPLICATION_JSON)
 @ClientHeaderParam(name = "User-Agent", value = "MicroProfile REST Client
1.2")
 Now tz(@PathParam("tz") String tz);
}
```

It is also possible to add or propagate headers in bulk using a `ClientHeadersFactory` implementation:

```
package org.eclipse.microprofile.rest.client.ext;

public interface ClientHeadersFactory {
 MultivaluedMap<String, String> update(
    MultivaluedMap<String, String> incomingHeaders,
    MultivaluedMap<String, String> clientOutgoingHeaders);
}
```

In the preceding code snippet, the `incomingHeaders` and `clientOutgoingHeaders` parameters are used as follows:

- `incomingHeaders`: Represents the map of headers for the inbound request
- `clientOutgoingHeaders`: Represents the read-only map of header values specified on the client interface, the union of header values from `@ClientHeaderParam`, `@HeaderParam`, and so on

The `update` method should return a `MultivaluedMap` that contains the headers to merge with the `clientOutgoingHeaders` map for the complete map of headers to be sent to the outbound request. Providers such as filters, interceptors, and message body writers could still modify the final map of headers prior to sending the HTTP request.

To enable a `ClientHeadersFactory`, the client interface must be annotated with the `@RegisterClientHeaders` annotation. If this annotation specifies a value, the client implementation must invoke an instance of the specified `ClientHeadersFactory` implementation class. If no value is specified, then the client implementation must invoke `DefaultClientHeadersFactoryImpl`. This default factory will propagate specified headers from the inbound JAX-RS request to the outbound request – these headers are specified with a comma-separated list using the MicroProfile Config property, `org.eclipse.microprofile.rest.client.propagateHeaders`.

# Provider registration for advanced usage

The `RestClientBuilder` interface extends the `Configurable` interface from JAX-RS, allowing a user to register custom providers while it is being built. The behavior of the providers supported is defined by the JAX-RS Client API specification. An MP-RC implementation will support `ClientResponseFilter`, `ClientRequestFilter`, `MessageBodyReader`, `MessageBodyWriter`, `ParamConverter`, `ReaderInterceptor`, and `WriterInterceptor` from JAX-RS.

For the `ClientResponseFilter` and `ClientRequestFilter` interfaces that have a `ClientRequestContext` parameter in their `filter` method, MP-RC implementations add an `org.eclipse.microprofile.rest.client.invokedMethod` property, the value of which is the `java.lang.reflect.Method` object representing the REST Client interface method currently being invoked.

In addition to defining providers via `RestClientBuilder`, interfaces may use the `@RegisterProvider` annotation to define classes to be registered as providers.

Providers may also be registered by implementing the `RestClientBuilderListener` or `RestClientListener` interfaces. These interfaces are intended as SPIs to allow global provider registration, and implementations of these interfaces must be specified in a `META-INF/services/org.eclipse.microprofile.rest.client.spi.RestClientBuilder Listener` or a `META-INF/services/org.eclipse.microprofile.rest.client.spi.RestClientListene r` file, respectively, following the `ServiceLoader` pattern.

# Provider priority

Providers may be registered via both annotations and `RestClientBuilder`. Providers registered via a builder will take precedence over the `@RegisterProvider` annotation. The `@RegisterProvider` annotation priority value takes precedence over any `@javax.annotation.Priority` annotation on the class. Provider priorities can be overridden when using the register methods on the `RestClientBuilder` interface as it allows for priority.

# Feature registration

If the type of provider registered is a JAX-RS `Feature`, then the priority set by that `Feature` will be part of the builder as well. Implementations maintain the overall priority of registered providers, regardless of how they are registered. `Feature` will be used to register additional providers at runtime, and may be registered via `@RegisterProvider`, configuration, or via `RestClientBuilder`. `Feature` will be executed immediately. As a result, its priority is not taken into account (features are always executed).

# Default providers

MP-RC implementations must provide a minimum set of providers, including the following:

- `*/json` types:
    - JSON-P, `javax.json.JsonValue`
    - JSON-B, `javax.json.bind`
- `*` types:
    - `byte[]`
    - `java.lang.String`
    - `java.io.InputStream`
    - `java.io.Reader`
- `text/plain` types:
    - `java.lang.Number and subtypes`
    - `int, long, float and double`
    - `java.lang.Character and char`
    - `java.lang.Boolean and boolean`

# Exception mapping

MP-RC provides support for mapping an invocation response into an exception via the `org.eclipse.microprofile.rest.client.ext.ResponseExceptionMapper` interface:

```
import javax.annotation.Priority;
import javax.ws.rs.Priorities;
import javax.ws.rs.core.MultivaluedMap;
import javax.ws.rs.core.Response;
import java.util.Optional;

public interface ResponseExceptionMapper<T extends Throwable> {
    int DEFAULT_PRIORITY = Priorities.USER;

    T toThrowable(Response response);

    default boolean handles(int status, MultivaluedMap<String, Object>
headers) {
        return status >= 400;
    }
```

```
    default int getPriority() {
        return
Optional.ofNullable(getClass().getAnnotation(Priority.class))
            .map(Priority::value)
            .orElse(DEFAULT_PRIORITY);
    }
}
```

Consider the following interface:

```
@Path("/")
public interface SomeService {
    @GET
    public String get() throws SomeException;
}
```

To map an error status code onto the application-specific SomeException value, you would need the following:

```
public class SomeExceptionExceptionMapper implements
ResponseExceptionMapper<SomeException> {

 @Override
 public SomeException toThrowable(Response response) {
    // Possibly get message from response...
     return new SomeException();
 }
}
```

Since the default ResponseExceptionMapper#handles() method returns true for any status code >= 400, this would be called to generate a SomeException value on any unsuccessful invocation of the SomeService#get() method.

# Default exception mapping

Each implementation provides a default ResponseExceptionMapper implementation that will map and invoke a response to javax.ws.rs.WebApplicationException when the response status code is >= 400. It has a priority of Integer.MAX_VALUE, and is meant to be used as a fallback whenever an error is encountered. This mapper will be registered by default to all client interfaces, but this can be disabled by setting an MP Config property, microprofile.rest.client.disable.default.mapper, to true. It can also be disabled on a per-client basis by using the same property when building the client:

```
RestClientBuilder.newBuilder().property("microprofile.rest.client.disable.d
efault.mapper",true)
```

# Async support

MP-RC supports asynchronous method invocations. A client interface method is asynchronous when the return type of the method is of the `java.util.concurrent.CompletionStage<?>` type. An alternative version, called `WorldClockApiAsync.java`, of the `WorldClockApi` interface that declares an asynchronous method is as follows:

```java
import java.util.concurrent.CompletionStage;

import javax.ws.rs.GET;
import javax.ws.rs.Path;
import javax.ws.rs.PathParam;
import javax.ws.rs.Produces;
import javax.ws.rs.core.MediaType;

@Path("/api/json")
public interface WorldClockApiAsync {
  String BASE_URL = "http://worldclockapi.com/api/json";

  @GET
  @Path("/utc/now")
  @Produces(MediaType.APPLICATION_JSON)
  CompletionStage<Now> utc();

  @GET
  @Path("{tz}/now")
  @Produces(MediaType.APPLICATION_JSON)
  CompletionStage<Now> tz(@PathParam("tz") String tz);
}
```

In this version, the `utc()` and `tz(String)` methods return `CompletionStage<Now>` types, so the MP-RC implementation will handle the request on one thread and the response on a different thread. It does not specify which thread providers on the outbound client request are run. A client may specify `java.util.concurrent.ExecutorService` to use for asynchronous processing. This is done using the `RestClient.executorService(ExecutorService)` method when building the client proxy. All asynchronous methods built using a given executor must be processed using that executor.

An example client of this `WorldClockApiAsync` interface is `WorldClockCDIAsyncUser.java`, which is illustrated as follows:

```java
@ApplicationScoped
@Path("/cdi-async")
public class WorldClockCDIAsyncUser {
```

```
@Inject
@RestClient
WorldClockApiAsync remoteApi;

    @GET
    @Path("/now-utc")
    @Produces(MediaType.TEXT_PLAIN)
    public Response getCurrentDateTime() {
        CompletionStage<Now> nowCS = remoteApi.utc();
        Now now = null;
        try {
            now = nowCS.toCompletableFuture().get();
        } catch (Exception e) {
            return Response.status(Response.Status.INTERNAL_SERVER_ERROR)
                .entity("Failed to : " + e.getMessage())
                .build();
        }
        return Response.ok(now.getCurrentDateTime()).build();
    }
}
```

Here, we have shown you support for asynchronous method invocation by MP-RC.

 The MP-RC project source code can be found at the following location: https://github.com/eclipse/microprofile-rest-client.

# Summary

In this chapter, we have learned about two Eclipse MicroProfile specifications, namely, Eclipse MicroProfile OpenAPI and Eclipse MicroProfile REST Client. The former provides a specification for generating OpenAPI-compliant documentation for your microservices, and the latter supplies a specification for calling REST endpoints in a type-safe manner. In this chapter, we covered the specific capabilities of these specifications, provided some example code, and supplied pointers on how to get further information about these specifications. You have learned the features and capabilities of the Eclipse MicroProfile OpenAPI and Eclipse MicroProfile REST Client specifications, how to use their annotations and programmatic interfaces, and how you could incorporate them into your applications.

In the next chapter, we will discuss and delve into the open source implementations of Eclipse MicroProfile that currently exist on the market.

# Questions

1. Do you need to do anything to get information supplied to the `/openapi` endpoint?
2. Can I enhance OpenAPI output with just one or two extra annotations?
3. What is the point of using static OpenAPI files?
4. Do I need the REST endpoint microservice I want to use to provide the MP-REST interface?
5. How do you externalize the base URL for a type-safe interface?
6. What if I need to propagate incoming request headers?

# Section 3: MicroProfile Implementations and Roadmap 3

This section goes over the current market implementations and a possible roadmap for future projects.

This section contains the following chapter:

- Chapter 7, *MicroProfile Implementations, Quarkus, and Interoperability via the Conference Application*

# 7
# MicroProfile Implementations, Quarkus, and Interoperability via the Conference Application

One of the benefits of Eclipse MicroProfile is that it provides a specification that allows many implementations to be interoperable with each other. This benefit has encouraged many vendors and community groups to implement the Eclipse MicroProfile specification as open source implementations. There are currently eight implementations of Eclipse MicroProfile in the market, with a ninth entrant, Quarkus.

The following topics will be covered in this chapter:

- A description of the eight implementations of Eclipse MicroProfile and how to find further information on each
- How to generate Eclipse MicroProfile sample code for each of these implementations
- A description of the ninth implementation of Eclipse MicroProfile, Quarkus
- A description of *The Conference Application*, an Eclipse MicroProfile interoperability proof-of-concept

# Current MicroProfile implementations

At the time of writing, there are eight implementations of Eclipse MicroProfile, all of which are open source. Here is a table of these implementations:

| Open source project basis | Project location | Supporting vendor |
|---|---|---|
| Thorntail (http://thorntail.io/) | https://github.com/thorntail/thorntail | Red Hat |
| Open Liberty (https://openliberty.io/) | https://github.com/openliberty | IBM |
| Apache TomEE (http://tomee.apache.org/) | https://github.com/apache/tomee | Tomitribe |
| Payara Micro (https://www.payara.fish/payara_micro) | https://github.com/payara/Payara | Payara Services Ltd. |
| Hammock (https://hammock-project.github.io/) | https://github.com/hammock-project | Hammock |
| KumuluzEE (https://ee.kumuluz.com/) | https://github.com/kumuluz | KumuluzEE |
| Launcher (https://github.com/fujitsu/launcher) | https://github.com/fujitsu/launcher | Fujitsu |
| Helidon (https://helidon.io/#) | https://github.com/oracle/helidon | Oracle |

Some of these implementations are based on *application servers*, such as Payara and Open Liberty, while others are based on *application assemblers* that include only the functionality that the application needs, instead of requiring an application server to be up and running, and commonly generate an executable JAR. However, the implementations based on application servers are also capable of producing executable JAR as well.

An application assembler can generate an *uberjar*, a self-contained runnable JAR file, or an *application jar* with its runtime dependencies located in a subdirectory, for example, an accompanying lib or libs subdirectory.

Eclipse MicroProfile implementations that pass the MicroProfile **Test Compatibility Kit** (**TCK**) for the entire umbrella release, or a specific version of a MicroProfile API are listed at https://wiki.eclipse.org/MicroProfile/Implementation. At the moment, inclusion in this list uses the honor system because it does not require proof of the TCK results; it just requires that the publishers assert that their implementation has passed the TCK.

The project also has a site where organizations/groups can self-include in the list of production deployments of MicroProfile. This list can be found at https://wiki.eclipse.org/MicroProfile/Adoptions.

In the next sections, we provide brief descriptions of these implementations and how to get more information on each of them.

# Thorntail

Red Hat are the sponsors of the open source Thorntail project, which implements the Eclipse MicroProfile specification. Thorntail is an application assembler that packages just the server runtime components required by your application and creates a runnable JAR (that is, an uberjar), which you can execute by invoking the following command:

```
$ java -jar <executable JAR file>
```

Not only is Thorntail MicroProfile-compatible, but it can also include functionality beyond MicroProfile in your application. It has the concept of a fraction, which is a specific library that contains functionality you want to include in your application. A fraction is included in the Maven POM file of your application as a dependency. Beyond the MicroProfile fraction, Thorntail provides fractions for OpenShift, Batch, Cassandra, data, encryption, monitoring, tracing, Hibernate, Fault Tolerance, Integration, Management, REST, NoSQL, Reactive, Security, Web, and more. For a list of valid fractions that can be used as dependencies, you can check the project's GitHub location at https://github.com/thorntail/thorntail/tree/master/fractions, or you can click on the **View all available dependencies** link in the Thorntail Generator, which we describe in the next paragraph.

The Thorntail Generator (`https://thorntail.io/generator/`) is a tool that allows you to create a sample *Hello World* executable JAR that includes all the fractions/dependencies you choose via its user interface, which is as follows:

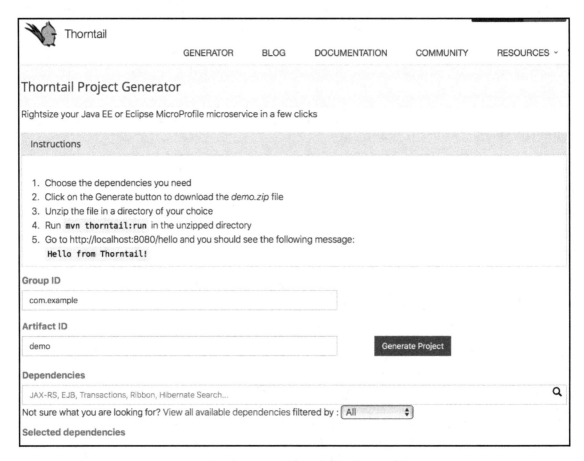

You can leave **Group ID** and **Artifact ID** with their default values and enter the fractions you would like to include as dependencies in your application in the field titled **Dependencies**, which has auto-complete capabilities as you type the dependency name. As mentioned in the previous paragraph, if you'd like to see all the available dependencies, click on the **View all available dependencies** link right under the **Dependencies** field.

Thorntail leverages SmallRye, an open source project that's a partial implementation of Eclipse MicroProfile. The idea of SmallRye is to develop code that can be reused across multiple implementations of MicroProfile. For example, in addition to Thorntail, SmallRye is also leveraged by other open source projects, such as WildFly and Quarkus.

For more information on SmallRye, please refer to `https://smallrye.io`.

Red Hat recently announced that it will be superseding Thorntail with Quarkus and WildFly. They will continue to offer production support for Thorntail until November 2020 to give ample time for customers to either migrate to Quarkus or WildFly.

 For more information on this announcement, refer to `https://thorntail.io/posts/thorntail-community-announcement-on-quarkus`.

Now, let's move on to the next implementation of MicroProfile in the market.

# Open Liberty

IBM are the sponsors of the open source Open Liberty project, which implements the Eclipse MicroProfile specification. Open Liberty is the upstream open source project for the IBM WebSphere Liberty application server. Open Liberty is an application server capable of generating an uberjar, which contains your application with an embedded Open Liberty server inside of it. To run the uberjar, you need to enter the following command:

```
$ java -jar <executable JAR file>
```

This command will explode the JAR file into your username's temporary directory, and then it will execute the application from there.

 Ensure there are no spaces in the path to the JAR file, otherwise the start up process will fail.

The generated uberjar can contain only a subset of application server functionality as defined by the features included in the `server.xml` file. To build an uberjar with this minimal set of features, you need to use the `minify-runnable-package` profile when running Maven.

The Open Liberty documentation is very thorough and replete with guides and reference documents.

You can find the Open Liberty documentation at `https://openliberty.io/docs/`.

In their documentation, they have a section dedicated to MicroProfile guides, which provide well-documented tutorials.

# Apache TomEE

Tomitribe are the sponsors of the open source TomEE project, which implements the Eclipse MicroProfile specification. Apache TomEE is assembled from Apache Tomcat with added Java EE features. TomEE is Java EE 6 Web Profile-certified. As its GitHub describes it, *Apache TomEE is a lightweight, yet powerful, JavaEE Application server with feature-rich tooling*. There are a few different versions of TomEE that you can download; for example, TomEE, TomEE+, and TomEE WebApp, but the one we are interested in is TomEE MicroProfile. For MicroProfile, TomEE generates an uberjar for your microservice, which you can run as follows:

```
$ java -jar <executable JAR file>
```

Although the TomEE MicroProfile documentation is scarce, a set of thorough MicroProfile examples are provided at the Apache TomEE documentation site.

To access the MicroProfile examples, go to the Apache TomEE documentation site at `http://tomee.apache.org/docs.html`, and select the *Examples* link under the latest release section.

Apache TomEE is often described as the Java Enterprise Edition of Apache Tomcat and as a MicroProfile-compliant application server.

# Payara Micro

Payara are the sponsors of the open source Payara Micro project, which implements the Eclipse MicroProfile specification. Payara Server is based on the open source application server, GlassFish. Payara Micro is based on Payara Server, albeit a slimmed-down version of it. As their website describes, *Payara Micro is the microservices-ready version of Payara Server*.

The way Payara Micro works is that a Payara Micro instance starts and then your MicroProfile microservice is deployed to it as a WAR file. For example, to start a Payara Micro instance, you would enter the following command:

```
$ java -jar payara-micro.jar
```

To start a Payara Micro instance and deploy your application to it, you would enter the following command:

```
$ java -jar payara-micro.jar --deploy <WAR file>
```

Payara Micro supports Java EE application deployments and it is also compatible with Eclipse MicroProfile.

 For the Payara Micro documentation, please refer to https://docs. payara.fish/documentation/payara-micro/payara-micro.html.

Lastly, Payara Micro supports automatic clustering by using a third-party in-memory data grid product.

# Hammock

John Ament is the sponsor of the open source Hammock project, which implements the Eclipse MicroProfile specification. Similar to Thorntail, Hammock is an application assembler that generates uberjars. To run the uberjar, you need to enter the following command:

```
$ java -jar <executable JAR file>
```

Hammock is an opinionated microservices framework for building applications. It is a CDI-based framework, meaning that it is on a CDI container with CDI-based beans that run in it. It supports two CDI implementations (JBoss Weld and Apache OpenWebBeans), three JAX-RS implementations (Apache CXF, Jersey, and JBoss RestEasy), and three different servlet containers (Apache Tomcat, JBoss Undertow, and Eclipse Jetty). Besides these, Hammock also supports other dependencies that you can bring into your application, such as Security, Metrics, Arquillian, and Apache ActiveMQ Artemis.

For the list of modules supported by Hammock, please refer to `https://github.com/hammock-project/hammock/wiki/Modules`.

Hammock strongly recommends using Capsule (`http://www.capsule.io`) to package your applications. In addition, it provides basic JPA support and its database migration capabilities are based on FlywayDB (`https://flywaydb.org`). Its documentation is a bit scarce, and despite not offering a sample project generator, it provides some simple examples on how to get started.

# KumuluzEE

Sunesis are the sponsors of the open source KumuluzEE project, which implements the Eclipse MicroProfile specification. KumuluzEE defines itself as a lightweight microservices framework using Java and Java EE technologies and as Eclipse MicroProfile-compliant implementation. KumuluzEE allows you to bootstrap a Java EE application using just the components that you need, and it also supports the packing and running microservices as uberjars. Just like other implementations that support uberjars, you can run your microservices by entering the following command:

```
$ java -jar <executable JAR file>
```

KumuluzEE also provides a POM generator that can create a `pom.xml` with the selected options and features you would like to include for the microservice you plan to develop. The POM generator provides a clear and organized list of profiles, components, and projects supported by KumuluzEE that you can select to include in the `pom.xml` file.

KumuluzEE provides a handful of samples for the different MicroProfile APIs.

For documentation related to the KumuluzEE implementation of Eclipse MicroProfile, refer to `https://ee.kumuluz.com/microprofile`.

Lastly, KumuluzEE provides some interesting tutorials at `https://ee.kumuluz.com/tutorials/`.

# Launcher

Fujitsu are the sponsors of the open source Launcher project, which implements the Eclipse MicroProfile specification. Launcher leverages an embedded GlassFish Server and Apache Geronimo MicroProfile API implementations. You can run your microservice as a WAR file, as follows:

```
$ java -jar launcher-1.0.jar --deploy my-app.war
```

In addition, Launcher can create uberjars. To create and run your microservice as an uberjar, first generate the uberjar and then invoke it using `java -jar`, as follows:

```
$ java -jar launcher-1.0.jar --deploy my-app.war --generate my-uber.jar
$ java -jar my-uber.jar
```

The documentation for Launcher is very scarce and limited. You can find usage information about Launcher at `https://github.com/fujitsu/launcher/blob/master/doc/Usage.adoc` and download it from `https://github.com/fujitsu/launcher/releases`.

# Helidon

Oracle Corporation are the sponsors of the open source Helidon project, which implements the Eclipse MicroProfile specification. Helidon is a set of Java libraries that enable a developer to write microservices. It leverages Netty, a non-blocking I/O client server framework. Helidon is an application assembler in that it generates application JAR. Once you have built the application JAR, you can execute it with the following command:

```
$ java -jar <executable JAR file>
```

Helidon comes in two flavors: SE and MP. Helidon SE is the functional programming style provided by all Helidon libraries and it provides a microservices framework called MicroFramework. Helidon MP implements the MicroProfile specification for microservices, and it's built on top of Helidon libraries. There is no sample project generator tool, but Helidon provides a rich and thorough set of documentation manuals.

 The documentation for Helidon can be found at `https://helidon.io/docs/latest/#/about/01_overview`.

Helidon SE provides a WebServer, which is an asynchronous and reactive API for creating web applications. Helidon MP provides a MicroProfile server implementation that encapsulates the Helidon WebServer.

# Generating sample code for the current implementations

As described in the previous sections, most MicroProfile implementations do not provide their own sample project generators. Instead, they just provide documentation. This is where the MicroProfile Starter comes to the rescue!

The MicroProfile Starter is sponsored by the MicroProfile community and is a tool that generates sample project and source code for the MicroProfile specifications for all of the MicroProfile implementations that have passed the MicroProfile TCK. In Chapter 2, *Governance and Contributions*, we gave you a tour of the MicroProfile Starter. To avoid being repetitive, we just want to point out that you can select the MicroProfile version in the drop-down menu as follows:

A list of MicroProfile implementations will appear on the drop-down list for MicroProfile implementations:

For example, if you select **MP 1.2** for the MicroProfile version, five implementations will be displayed (in random order) for MicroProfile servers, for which the MicroProfile Starter can generate sample source code and projects. In this example, TomEE, Thorntail, KumuluzEE, Open Liberty, and Helidon are the implementations that support MicroProfile 1.2. The generated ZIP file will contain a README file that contains instructions on how to build and run the generated project for the specific MicroProfile server you selected.

## Other projects that implement MicroProfile

SmallRye is an open source project that develops implementations of Eclipse MicroProfile usable by any vendor or project. It's a community effort and everyone is welcome to participate and contribute to SmallRye, `https://smallrye.io`. As an example of this, the community recently contributed the Extensions for MicroProfile project into SmallRye, hence enriching its functionality with extensions for Config Sources, OpenAPI, Health, JAX-RS, and REST Client.

 The Extensions for MicroProfile project website is `https://www.microprofile-ext.org`, and its GitHub is `https://github.com/microprofile-extensions`.

SmallRye implementations are tested against, and have passed, the Eclipse MicroProfile TCKs.

Open source projects that consume SmallRye are Thorntail (`https://thorntail.io`), WildFly (`https://wildfly.org`), and Quarkus (`https://quarkus.io`).

## Quarkus

The open source Quarkus project made its debut in 2019. Quarkus is a Kubernetes-native Java stack with that can compile to native machine language or building to HotSpot (OpenJDK). When using Quarkus, your application consumes very little memory, has great performance that allows it to handle a high throughput of invocations, and has a very fast start up time (that is, boot plus first response time), making Quarkus a great runtime for containers, as well as cloud-native and serverless deployments. Quarkus also provides an extension framework that allows the *quarking* of libraries and projects to make them work seamlessly with Quarkus.

Quarkus's mission is to transform your full application and the libraries it uses into an optimal output for GraalVM. To do this, you need to analyze and understand the full *closed world* of the application. Without the full and complete context, the best that can be achieved is partial and limited generic support. By using the Quarkus extension approach, we can bring high density to Java applications.

The Quarkus extension framework makes a significant impact even when GraalVM is not used (for example in HotSpot). Let's list the actions an extension perform:

1.  An extension hosts code substitution so that libraries can run on GraalVM:
    *   Most changes are pushed upstream to help the underlying library run on GraalVM.
    *   Not all changes can be pushed upstream; extensions host code substitutions – which is a form of code patching – so that libraries can run.

2.  An extension host code substitution to help dead code elimination based on the requirements of the application:
    *   This is application-dependent and cannot really be shared in the library itself.
    *   For example, Quarkus optimizes the Hibernate code because it knows it only needs a specific connection pool and cache provider.

3.  An extension gather build time metadata and generates code:
    *   This part has nothing to do with GraalVM; it is how Quarkus starts frameworks *at build time*.
    *   The extension framework facilitates the reading of metadata, scanning classes, and generating classes as needed.

4.  An extension send metadata to GraalVM for classes in need of reflection:
    *   This information is not static per library (for example, Hibernate), but the framework has the semantic knowledge and knows which classes need to have reflection (for example, `@Entity` classes)

5.  An extension offers an opinionated choice based on the close world view of the application, including configuration.

All the preceding steps are done at build time and not runtime. This is what is known as *compile-time boot*.

As an example of what extensions do, the Quarkus Arc extension (our CDI injection facility) generates direct bytecode to wire your components together. This means that if you have three candidate beans to resolve an injection point, we do not resolve this at runtime (as traditionally done in Java). We instead solve this at build time and transform your application to directly instantiate the correct bean. This type of code is easy for a static compiler such as GraalVM to determine what precise code can be eliminated. Without this type of work, GraalVM would have to assume all three beans were needed.

The Quarkus project welcomes and encourages other open source projects to quark their libraries. In fact, this is how Eclipse MicroProfile is included as part of the Java stack included with Quarkus. Some community-quarked projects include swagger-ui, Flyway, and R-script, among others.

As a Java stack, it supports many Java libraries, one of them being Eclipse MicroProfile.

 For more information on Quarkus, refer to its website, `https://quarkus.io`.

Quarkus has many get-started examples, as well as numerous guides. You can find them at `https://quarkus.io/guides/`. In addition, you can find a lot of informational videos at the Quarkus YouTube channel, which features *Quarkus Tips* or Q-tips, which are short 5-minute videos on a variety of Quarkus topics.

Earlier in this chapter, we covered how to generate sample MicroProfile code by using the MicroProfile Starter. As you probably may have noticed by now, Quarkus was not one of the possible MicroProfile servers listed in the MicroProfile Starter. At the time of writing, Quarkus is still in Beta, so the MicroProfile Starter development team will take it up and support it once Quarkus releases its first GA release. However, this doesn't stop you from quarking a project generated by the MicroProfile Starter today. The next section goes over the steps to do just that.

# How to quark a generated MicroProfile project

Before we start with the steps on how to *quark* a generated MicroProfile project by the MicroProfile Starter, we need to first make sure to have GRAALVM_HOME installed, defined, and configured in your environment. To this end, follow these steps:

1. Go to `https://github.com/oracle/graal/releases` and download the latest release of GraalVM for your operating system.

2. Unzip the downloaded file into a sub-directory of your choosing. By the way, the unzipping will create a sub-directory for GraalVM, /Users/[YOUR HOME DIRECTORY]/graalvm-ce-1.0.0-rc13, for example:

```
$ cd $HOME
$ tar -xzf graalvm-ce-1.0.0-rc16-macos-amd64.tar.gz
```

3. Open a terminal window and create an environment variable called GRAALVM_HOME, for example:

```
$ export GRAALVM_HOME=/Users/[YOUR HOME DIRECTORY]/graalvm-
ce-1.0.0-rc13/Contents/Home
```

Now that we have installed GraalVM, we can move on to the steps on how to *quark* a generated MicroProfile project with MicroProfile Starter:

1. First, point your browser to https://start.microprofile.io and select Thorntail as the MicroProfile Server.

> You can leverage the following steps to *quark* any existing Java application as well.

> If you don't recall how to do this, go to Chapter 2, *Governance and Contributions*, and follow the instructions in the *Quick tour of the MicroProfile Starter* section up to step 5, where the demo.zip file is downloaded to your local Downloads directory.

2. Expand the demo.zip file that the MicroProfile Starter generated under your Downloads local directory using your favorite unzipping tool. If your demo.zip file didn't get automatically expanded, here are the commands to do it (assuming Linux; for Windows, please use the equivalent commands):

```
$ cd $HOME/Downloads
$ unzip demo.zip
```

This will create a demo sub-directory with an entire directory tree structure under it with all the source files needed to build and run the Thorntail sample MicroProfile project using Maven.

3. Instead of making changes in the demo sub-directory, let's create a second directory called Qproj4MP alongside the demo sub-directory, as follows:

```
$ mkdir $HOME/Downloads/Qproj4MP
```

This should create a sub-directory called `Qproj4MP` at the same level as your existing `demo` sub-directory in your `Downloads` directory.

4. Change your directory to `Qproj4MP` and create an empty Quarkus project by entering the following commands:

```
$ cd $HOME/Downloads/Qproj4MP
$ mvn io.quarkus:quarkus-maven-plugin:0.12.0:create \
 -DprojectGroupId=com.example \
 -DprojectArtifactId=demo \
 -Dextensions="smallrye-health, smallrye-metrics, smallrye-openapi,
smallrye-fault-tolerance, smallrye-jwt, resteasy, resteasy-jsonb,
arc"
```

5. Within the `Qproj4MP` directory, delete the `src` sub-directory and replace it with the `src` sub-directory from the Thorntail sample MicroProfile project by entering the following commands:

```
$ cd $HOME/Downloads/Qproj4MP  # ensuring you are in the Qproj4MP
sub-directory
$ rm -rf ./src
$ cp -pR $HOME/Downloads/demo/src .
```

6. Quarkus and Thorntail differ in their expectations of where some configuration and web app-related files need to be. So, in order to make Quarkus happy, let's copy some files around by entering the following commands:

```
$ cd $HOME/Downloads/Qproj4MP # ensuring you are in the Qproj4MP
sub-directory
$ mkdir src/main/resources/META-INF/resources
$ cp /Users/csaavedr/Downloads/demo/src/main/webapp/index.html
src/main/resources/META-INF/resources
$ cp -p src/main/resources/META-INF/microprofile-config.properties
src/main/resources/application.properties
```

We could have moved these files from their original locations, but we chose to just copy them for this example.

7. The Thorntail sample MicroProfile project that was generated by MicroProfile Starter and whose `src` sub-directory contents you copied to `Qproj4MP` uses a security library called `bouncycastle`. The reason for this is that the generated code includes an example for the MicroProfile JWT Propagation specification, which allows you propagate security across microservices. Because of this, we also need to add two more dependencies to the Quarkus project POM file, one for `bouncycastle` and one for `nimbusds`.

The `bouncycastle` dependency will be removed from the Thorntail server code generation in the next sprint release of MicroProfile Starter.

To add these dependencies, edit the `pom.xml` file under your `$HOME/Downloads/Qproj4MP` directory and, in the section for `<dependencies>`, enter the following code block:

```
<dependency>
<groupId>org.bouncycastle</groupId>
<artifactId>bcpkix-jdk15on</artifactId>
<version>1.53</version>
<scope>test</scope>
</dependency>
<dependency>
<groupId>com.nimbusds</groupId>
<artifactId>nimbus-jose-jwt</artifactId>
<version>6.7</version>
<scope>test</scope>
</dependency>
```

We are now ready to compile the quarked MicroProfile project.

8. In addition to supporting building a Java project to run on OpenJDK, Quarkus supports compiling a Java project all the way down to machine code. Enter the following command to compile the quarked sample project to native code:

```
$ cd $HOME/Downloads/Qproj4MP # ensuring you are in the Qproj4MP
sub-directory
$ ./mvnw package -Pnative
```

9. To run the application, enter the following command:

```
$ ./target/demo-1.0-SNAPSHOT-runner
```

To test the application, please follow the instructions listed in Chapter 2, *Governance and Contributions*, in the *Quick tour of MicroProfile Starter* section, starting at step 10.

10. If you'd like to run the quarked project in development mode, first stop the running process and then enter the following commands:

```
$ cd $HOME/Downloads/Qproj4MP # ensuring you are in the Qproj4MP
sub-directory
$ ./mvnw compile quarkus:dev
```

At this point, you can open up the project with an IDE of your choice, such as Visual Studio Code or Eclipse IDE, and start making changes to the source code. Quarkus supports hot reloads, meaning that, as soon as you make any changes to the source code, Quarkus rebuilds and redeploys your application in the background so that you can immediately see and test the effect of the changes. In addition, if you make a syntactical mistake in your source code, Quarkus will propagate meaningful error messages to the web app to help you fix your errors, making you more productive.

11. If you'd like to generate an executable application JAR, enter the following commands:

```
$ cd $HOME/Downloads/Qproj4MP # ensuring you are in the Qproj4MP
sub-directory
$ ./mvn clean package
```

12. To run the executable application JAR, enter the following command:

```
$ java -jar target/demo-1.0-SNAPSHOT-runner.jar
```

A lib directory is created alongside the application JAR with the library files it needs to run.

We have shown you the steps to *quark* a MicroProfile project generated by MicroProfile Starter. Although these steps apply to a specific generated project, you could use the same instructions to *quark* an existing Java application or microservice so that you can take advantage of the benefits that Quarkus provides, such as low memory consumption, fast start up time, and native compilation of your Java code so that you can run it efficiently in containers, the cloud, and Function-as-a-Service environments. No matter which implementation of MicroProfile you are using, a big benefit that MicroProfile provides to end users is interoperability. This means that you can design an application with microservices that use different implementations of MicroProfile, which is the topic of the following section.

# MicroProfile interoperability – the conference application

The **Conference Application**, first presented (https://www.youtube.com/watch?v=iG-XvoIfKtg) during Devoxx Belgium in November 2016, is a MicroProfile demo that showcases the integration and interoperability of different MicroProfile vendor implementations. This is important because it demonstrates the separation between implementation and interfaces of the specification, which provides a platform that allows vendors to develop and provide their own implementation that could coexist side by side with other competing implementations. The common interfaces across all implementations also provided end users with the benefit of flexibility and choice to use whichever MicroProfile implementation(s) makes the most sense for them. This interoperability also supports the notion of microservices and microservices architectures, in that each microservice could use any underlying technology and could be a cog in a larger application by means of its common interfaces, that is, API-based endpoints. So, let's delve into the structure of this demo that drives the very important interoperability aspect of MicroProfile. The demo consists of four microservices, each developed by a different vendor implementation of MicroProfile. This demo application (https://github.com/eclipse/microprofile-conference) is maintained by the community.

The **Conference Application** mimics an application used by the attendees of a technical conference to do the following:

- See a list of sessions to attend (Session microservice)
- See a list of speakers delivering sessions (Speaker microservice)
- Schedule sessions to attend (Schedule microservice)
- Vote for a session (Vote microservice)

The application also has a web app component as a frontend user interface that directly subscribes to each of the microservices.

Here is a diagram of the architecture of The Conference Application:

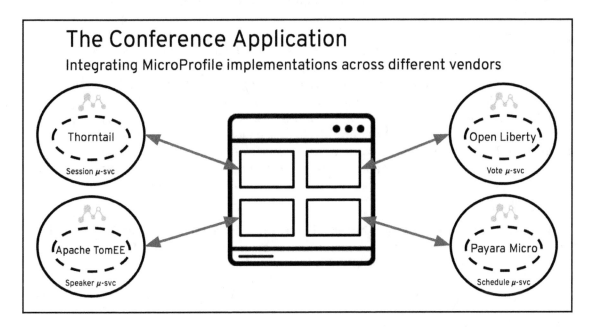

The following table summarizes each microservice, its underlying open source implementation, and the vendor that developed the microservice business logic:

| Microservice name | Description | Open source implementation | Vendor |
|---|---|---|---|
| microservice-session | The Session microservice lists available conference sessions. | Thorntail | Red Hat |
| microservice-schedule | The Schedule microservice allows the scheduling of conference sessions. | Payara Micro | Payara Services Ltd. |
| microservice-speaker | The Speaker microservice lists conference session speakers. | Apache TomEE | Tomitribe |
| microservice-vote | The Vote microservice allows the user to vote for conference sessions. | Open Liberty | IBM |

The beauty of microservices is that they communicate via their APIs using standard message formats, such as XML and JSON, and standard protocols, such as web services and REST. This permits an application to leverage microservices without caring about the programming language or underlying framework that the microservice is using for its implementation. Microservices implemented using the Eclipse MicroProfile specification have these characteristics. The Conference Application demonstrates the power of Eclipse MicroProfile APIs, which permit microservices developed by different implementations of the MicroProfile specification to be integral parts of an application by interoperating seamlessly with each other using standard mechanisms for transport and message communication and security, for example. This is a concrete expression of how microservices must work in a microservices architecture to instantiate a 12-factor application. The Conference Application is an insightful and preponderant example of the practicality, ease, and usability of a specification that is supported and developed by the community and for the community.

In the next chapter, you will find the resources to download, build, and run an adapted version of The Conference Application, which has been updated and enriched with the latest versions of the MicroProfile APIs.

# Summary

In this chapter, we have learned about the open source MicroProfile implementations that currently exist on the market, what types of implementation they are, how to get more information about each of them, and how to generate sample code for these implementations using MicroProfile Starter. We have also covered the latest MicroProfile implementation entrant, Quarkus, which introduces significant improvements to Java in start up time and memory consumption in interpreted and compiled modes, improving MicroProfile for cloud-native microservices and serverless environments even more. You also learned about The Conference Application, which demonstrates the interoperability of MicroProfile across different implementations.

As a consumer of Eclipse MicroProfile and its nature of being interoperable across implementations, you have the freedom to select the implementation that makes the most sense to your organization or is the best fit for your environment, ultimately giving you the option to choose the right tool for the right task. Moreover, you don't need to be stuck with a single vendor for a commercially supported version of Eclipse MicroProfile, and, as a result of this, you have the advantage to negotiate on your terms and select from a rich set of MicroProfile features offered by different vendors.

In the next chapter, we will cover a full code sample for the entire set of MicroProfile APIs.

# Questions

1. At present, how many implementations of MicroProfile exist in the market? List them.
2. What is the difference between an application server and an application assembler?
3. Describe each of the eight implementations of MicroProfile that exist in the market.
4. What is Quarkus?
5. What is compile-time boot?
6. What types of deployment is Quarkus a great runtime for?
7. What is the Quarkus extension framework?
8. What is the key benefit that The Conference Application demonstrates?

# 4

# Section 4: A Working MicroProfile Example

This section goes over an application that showcases MicroProfile.

This section contains the following chapter:

- Chapter 8, *A Working Eclipse MicroProfile Code Sample*

# A Working Eclipse MicroProfile Code Sample

**8**

In this chapter, we will discuss a sample application that makes use of the various MicroProfile features introduced earlier in this book. The MicroProfile runtime we will use in this chapter is the Quarkus runtime, a Kubernetes-native Java stack tailored for GraalVM and OpenJDK HotSpot, crafted from best of breed Java libraries and standards. Key topics that we will cover include the following:

- Use of configuration for both application and MicroProfile container behaviors
- Realistic health checks
- Securing an application with an external JWT security provider
- Integrating and viewing trace information with a Jaeger instance
- Inspecting microservice endpoint information using Swagger
- Viewing individual and complete application metrics
- Accessing both intra-cloud and external microservices using the `rest` client

The purpose of these topics is to provide you with a realistic overview of a non-trivial MicroProfile application that you can run and experiment with.

## Technical requirements

For this chapter, we'll require the following:

- An IDE
- JDK 1.8+ installed with `JAVA_HOME` configured appropriately
- Apache Maven 3.5.3+
- A running Docker environment

The code for this chapter can be found at `https://github.com/PacktPublishing/Hands-On-Enterprise-Java-Microservices-with-Eclipse-MicroProfile/tree/master/Chapter08-mpcodesample`.

The sample in this chapter can be compiled into a native binary using the GraalVM (`https://github.com/oracle/graal/releases/tag/vm-1.0.0-rc16`) integration of Quarkus. This has additional requirements for the installation of the 1.0-RC16 version Graal VM and a working C development environment. The details of the native image generation requirements can be found at `https://quarkus.io/guides/building-native-image-guide`.

# Sample architecture of a multiservice MicroProfile application

The sample application we will go over in this chapter is composed of an HTML frontend, two MicroProfile-based microservices, two external services we spin up using Docker, and an external time service on the web we have no control over. The architecture of our sample application is shown in the following diagram:

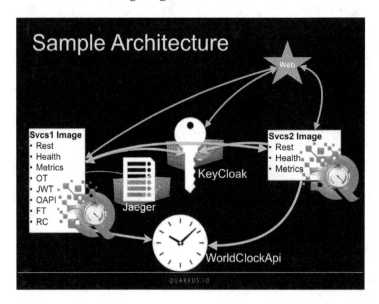

The key elements in this diagram include the following:

- **Svcs1 Image**: This is a collection of REST endpoints that make use of MP-HC, MP-Metrics, MP-OT, MP-JWT, MP-OAPI, MP-FT, and MP-RC in a Quarkus runtime.
- **Svcs2 Image**: This is a collection of REST endpoints that make use of MP-HC and MP-Metrics in a Quarkus runtime.
- **Jaeger**: This a Docker image that runs the Jaeger server for the collection of trace loggings.
- **KeyCloak**: This is a Docker image that runs a KeyCloak 6.0.0 server instance.
- **WorldClock**: This is an external service on the web that exposes an endpoint for the current date-time.
- **Web**: This is an HTML/CSS/Bootstrap frontend that accesses the Svcs1, Svcs2, and KeyCloak deployments running in a Quarkus runtime.

 For more information on the Quarkus runtime, visit the `https://quarkus.io/` website.

# Running the sample application

The sample application is designed to be run from four different shells, so let's organize them into four shell windows, as shown here:

| Docker Shell | Web Shell |
|---|---|
| Svcs1 Shell | Svcs2 Shell |

In each shell, run the commands as outlined in the correspondingly named sections that follow.

# The Docker shell commands

A common way to provide preconfigured servers/services is to use a Docker image that contains the service and all of its dependencies. In this example, we use Docker to run KeyCloak and Jaeger images. If you are not familiar with Docker or do not have the `docker` command installed, see the instructions for how to install Docker for your platform (`https://docs.docker.com/v17.12/install/`).

This project depends on KeyCloak for the MP-JWT token generation. To launch KeyCloak in a Docker container, run the following command in your shell:

```
docker run -d --name keycloak -e KEYCLOAK_USER=admin -e
KEYCLOAK_PASSWORD=admin -p 8180:8180 -v `pwd`/packt-mp-
realm.json:/config/quarkus-packt.json -it jboss/keycloak:6.0.1 -b 0.0.0.0
-Djboss.http.port=8180 -Dkeycloak.migration.action=import
-Dkeycloak.migration.provider=singleFile
-Dkeycloak.migration.file=/config/quarkus-packt.json
-Dkeycloak.migration.strategy=OVERWRITE_EXISTING
```

This project also depends on Jaeger for the collection of the MP OpenTracing information. To launch the Jaeger tracing system in a Docker container, run the following command:

```
docker run -d -e COLLECTOR_ZIPKIN_HTTP_PORT=9411 -p 5775:5775/udp -p
6831:6831/udp -p 6832:6832/udp -p 5778:5778 -p 16686:16686 -p 14268:14268 -
p 9411:9411 jaegertracing/all-in-one:latest
```

Once you have executed those commands, you can check the status of the Docker image startup using the `docker ps` command. Running that will produce something like the following:

```
Scotts-iMacPro:Chapter08-mpcodesample starksm$ docker ps
CONTAINER ID          IMAGE                               COMMAND
CREATED               STATUS               PORTS
NAMES
0202385b4076          jaegertracing/all-in-one:latest     "/go/bin/all-in-one-
..."     10 seconds ago       Up 9 seconds            0.0.0.0:5775->5775/udp,
0.0.0.0:5778->5778/tcp, 0.0.0.0:9411->9411/tcp, 0.0.0.0:14268->14268/tcp,
0.0.0.0:6831-6832->6831-6832/udp, 0.0.0.0:16686->16686/tcp, 14250/tcp
reverent_williamson
68c0b51f78b3          jboss/keycloak:6.0.1
"/opt/jboss/tools/do..."     22 seconds ago       Up 21 seconds            8080/tcp,
0.0.0.0:8180->8180/tcp
keycloak
```

With those images running, we have set up the KeyCloak instance we will use to secure our microservices using MP-JWT and the Jaeger instance we will use to capture and inspect the MP-OT traces. Next, we will bring up the first MicroProfile microservice instance.

# The Svcs1 shell command

Next, in the Svcs1 Terminal window you were asked to open earlier, navigate to the svcs1 subdirectory of the project and then run the following command to execute the svcs1 image in development mode:

```
mvn compile quarkus:dev
```

You will see the following output:

```
Scotts-iMacPro:svcs1 starksm$ mvn compile quarkus:dev
[INFO] Scanning for projects...
...
20:56:27 INFO [io.quarkus]] (main) Quarkus 0.15.0 started in 2.492s.
Listening on: http://[::]:8081
20:56:27 INFO [io.quarkus]] (main) Installed features: [cdi, jaeger,
resteasy, resteasy-jsonb, security, smallrye-fault-tolerance, smallrye-
health, smallrye-jwt, smallrye-metrics, smallrye-openapi, smallrye-
opentracing, smallrye-rest-client, swagger-ui]
```

In the output, we see that this instance is listening on the 8081 port for HTTP requests, and we see various Quarkus features that are installed to support our MicroProfile feature usage.

# The Svcs2 shell command

Next, in the Svcs2 Terminal window you were asked to open earlier, cd to the svcs2 subdirectory of the project and then run the following command to build the svcs2 image:

```
mvn clean package
```

Once the build is finished, to run the svcs2 JAR, enter the following command:

```
java -jar target/sample-svcs2-runner.jar
```

You will get the following output:

```
Scotts-iMacPro:svcs2 starksm$ java -jar target/sample-svcs2-runner.jar
...
20:58:55 INFO [io.quarkus]] (main) Quarkus 0.15.0 started in 0.936s.
Listening on: http://[::]:8082
20:58:55 INFO [io.quarkus]] (main) Installed features: [cdi, jaeger,
resteasy, resteasy-jsonb, security, smallrye-health, smallrye-jwt,
smallrye-metrics, smallrye-opentracing, smallrye-rest-client]
```

Here, we see that this image is listening on the 8082 port for HTTP requests, and we see the roughly the same set of Quarkus features as we did in the svcs1 image.

## The web shell command

Next, in the web shell Terminal window you were asked to open, clone this project to your computer, cd to the web subdirectory, and then run the following command to execute the web application in development mode:

```
mvn clean package
```

Once the build is finished, to run the web subproject JAR, enter the following:

```
java -jar target/sample-web-runner.jar
```

Once the application is up and running, point your browser to the web application at http://localhost:8080/index.html. In the next section, we will go over the web application details.

# Details of the sample application

Let's discuss in detail the various tabs in our application.

## The Config tab

The initial view of the application shows the **Config** tab, as shown in the following screenshot:

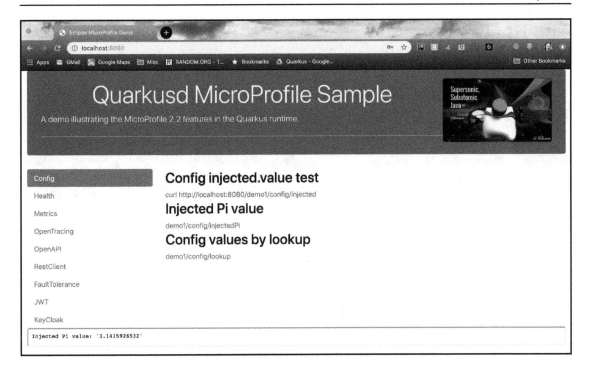

The three links are on the page reference endpoints in the
io.packt.sample.config.ConfigTestController class of the Chapter08-
mpcodesample/svcs1 subproject. Clicking on the various links displays the MP-Config
values. The value displayed in the previous screenshot corresponds to the second link and
the injected.piValue config value. The relevant settings from Chapter08-
mpcodesample/svcs1/src/main/resources/application.properties are shown
here:

```
# MP Config values for ConfigTestController
injected.value=Injected value
injected.piValue=3.1415926532
lookup.value=A Lookup value
```

Of note here is the override of the default five-digit value set via
the @ConfigProperty(name = "injected.piValue", defaultValue =
"pi5=3.14159") annotation in ConfigTestController to the full 10-digit value of PI as
seen in the previous screenshot.

# The Health tab

Clicking on the **Health** tab of the application displays a page like the following:

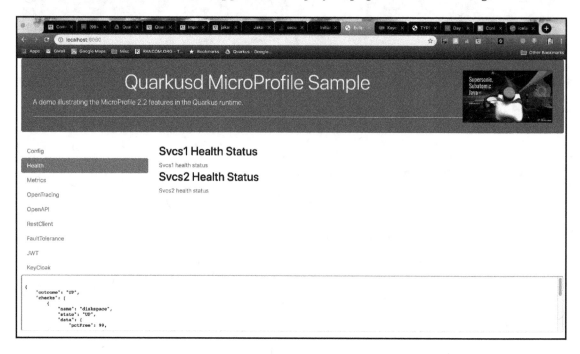

The links on the page correspond to the health check endpoints for the svcs1 and svcs2 images. Selecting either shows the health check output from the image. The svcs1 image health check is composed of the io.packt.sample.health.ServiceHealthCheck and io.packt.sample.health.CheckDiskspace. Furthermore, ServiceHealthCheck is just a mock implementation that always returns an up status. The CheckDiskspace health check procedure looks to a path set using the MP-Config health.pathToMonitor property and then sets the procedure status to up/down, based on whether or not the filesystem containing the path has free space greater or equal to the configured health.freeSpaceThreshold property.

The following snippet from Chapter08-mpcodesample/svcs1/src/main/resources/application.properties shows the values that are used to configure CheckDiskspace as found in the code repository:

```
# Diskspace health check properties
health.pathToMonitor=/Users/starksm
health.freeSpaceThreshold=1073741824
```

Now `health.pathToMonitor` is unlikely to exist on your system, so the health check output should be something like the following

where `health.pathToMonitor=/tmp/bad-path` refers to an invalid path:

```
{
    "outcome": "DOWN",
    "checks": [
        {
            "name": "diskspace",
            "state": "DOWN",
            "data": {
                "pctFree": 0,
                "path": "/tmp/bad-path",
                "exits": false,
                "freeSpace": 0,
                "usableSpace": 0
            }
        },
        {
            "name": "service-check",
            "state": "UP",
            "data": {
                "hostname": "service.jboss.com",
                "port": 12345,
                "isSecure": true
            }
        }
    ]
}
```

The `CheckDiskspace` code that manages the check is shown here:

```
@Health
@ApplicationScoped
public class CheckDiskspace implements HealthCheck {
    @Inject
    @ConfigProperty(name = "health.pathToMonitor")
    String pathToMonitor;
    @Inject
    @ConfigProperty(name = "health.freeSpaceThreshold")
    long freeSpaceThreshold;

    @Override
    public HealthCheckResponse call() {
        HealthCheckResponseBuilder builder =
HealthCheckResponse.named("diskspace");
        checkDiskspace(builder);
        return builder.build();
```

```
    }

    private void checkDiskspace(HealthCheckResponseBuilder builder) {
        File root = new File(pathToMonitor);
        long usableSpace = root.getUsableSpace();
        long freeSpace = root.getFreeSpace();
        long pctFree = 0;
        if (usableSpace > 0) {
            pctFree = (100 * usableSpace) / freeSpace;
        }
        builder.withData("path", root.getAbsolutePath())
                .withData("exits", root.exists())
                .withData("usableSpace", usableSpace)
                .withData("freeSpace", freeSpace)
                .withData("pctFree", pctFree)
                .state(freeSpace >= freeSpaceThreshold);
    }
}
```

The checkDiskspace method checks the configured path and validates if its freeSpace is more than or equal to the configured freeSpace threshold. It then adds a number of data items to indicate the reason for the health check status. Update the health.pathToMonitor property to point to a valid path on your system, then rebuild the svcs1 image and restart it. Alternatively, you could simply run the svcs1 image and override the health.pathToMonitor property via a system property like this:

```
mvn compile quarkus:dev -Dhealth.pathToMonitor=/mypath
```

Do this and then click on the **Svcs1 health status** link again. This time, you should see an UP status on the check with information about your selected path included in the reply.

## The Metrics tab

The **Metrics** tab shows the following view containing three links:

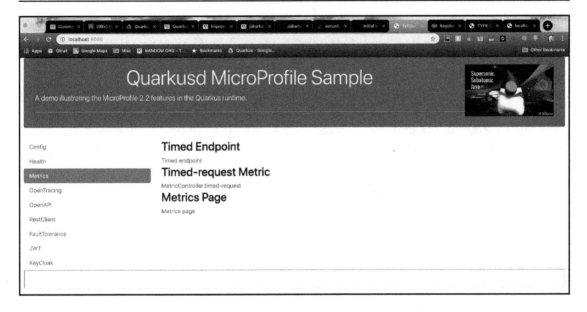

The first link accesses the following endpoint in the
`io.packt.sample.metric.MetricController` class:

```
@Path("timed")
@Timed(name = "timed-request")
@GET
@Produces(MediaType.TEXT_PLAIN)
public String timedRequest() {
    long start = System.currentTimeMillis();
    // Demo, not production style
    int wait = new Random().nextInt(1000);
    try {
        Thread.sleep(wait);
    } catch (InterruptedException e) {
        // Demo
        e.printStackTrace();
    }
    long end = System.currentTimeMillis();
    long delay = end - start;

    doIncrement();
    long count = getCustomerCount();
    return String.format("MetricController#timedRequest, delay[0-1000]=%d,
    count=%d", delay, count);
}
```

This annotates the `timed` path endpoint with an `@Timed(name = "timed-request")` annotation. This method uses a random delay between 0-1,000 ms to generate a distribution of response times. The next link is a direct link to the application-level metric for the `timedRequest()` method. The MP-Metrics specification defines the path as `metrics/application/io.packt.sample.metric.MetricController.timed-request`. After a few accesses to the first link to generate a range of response times, accessing the second link to retrieve the `timedRequest()` method metric will show something like the following:

```
# TYPE
application:io_packt_sample_metric_metric_controller_timed_request_rate_per
_second gauge
application:io_packt_sample_metric_metric_controller_timed_request_rate_per
_second 0.4434851530761856
# TYPE
application:io_packt_sample_metric_metric_controller_timed_request_one_min_
rate_per_second gauge
application:io_packt_sample_metric_metric_controller_timed_request_one_min_
rate_per_second 0.552026648777594
...
# TYPE
application:io_packt_sample_metric_metric_controller_timed_request_seconds
summary
application:io_packt_sample_metric_metric_controller_timed_request_seconds_
count 6.0
application:io_packt_sample_metric_metric_controller_timed_request_seconds{
quantile="0.5"} 0.923901552
...
application:io_packt_sample_metric_metric_controller_timed_request_seconds{
quantile="0.999"} 0.970502841
```

This is the range of information that the `@Timed` style of metric generates. The final link accesses the `metrics` endpoint that returns all of the metrics available in the image.

# The OpenTracing tab

The **OpenTracing** tab shows the following view with two links:

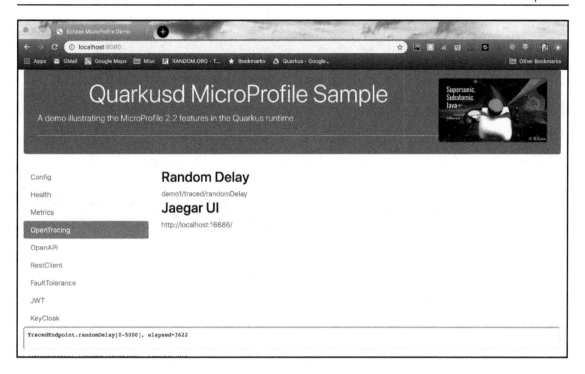

The first link accesses the following `io.packt.sample.tracing.TracedEndpoint` method:

```java
@GET
@Path("/randomDelay")
@Produces(MediaType.TEXT_PLAIN)
@Traced(operationName = "TracedEndpoint#demoRandomDelay")
public String randomDelay() {
    long start = System.currentTimeMillis();
    // 0-5 seconds random sleep
    long sleep = Math.round(Math.random() * 5000);
    try {
        Thread.sleep(sleep);
    } catch (InterruptedException e) {
        e.printStackTrace();
    }
    long end = System.currentTimeMillis();
    return String.format("TracedEndpoint.randomDelay[0-5000], elapsed=%d",
    (end - start));
}
```

The method uses a random delay between 0-5,000 ms to generate a range of response times. It is marked with the MP-OT `@Traced(operationName = "TracedEndpoint#demoRandomDelay")` annotation that assigns the `TracedEndpoint#demoRandomDelay` name to the trace operation.

The second link opens the Jaeger UI. If you open this link after clicking on the endpoint link for `randomDelay` and then navigate to the traces under the `QuarkusMPDemo` service, you will see something similar to the following view showing the `TracedEndpoint#demoRandomDelay` traces:

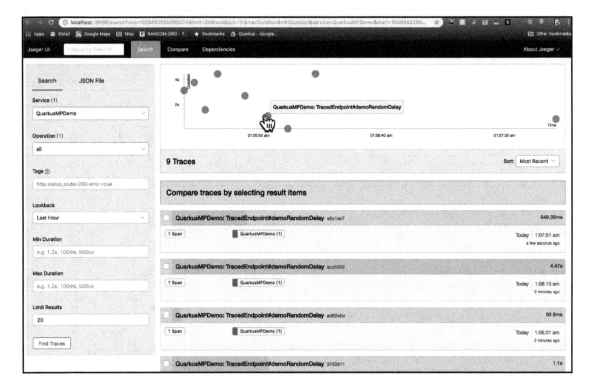

Hovering over the various circles in the graph gives the name of the trace. The range of the response times for the `TracedEndpoint#demoRandomDelay` method lies within the 0-5,000 ms range as we expect. As you continue through the application links, you can return to the Jaeger UI to view how the traces are recorded.

# The OpenAPI tab

The **OpenAPI** tab view contains two links and is as shown in the following screenshot:

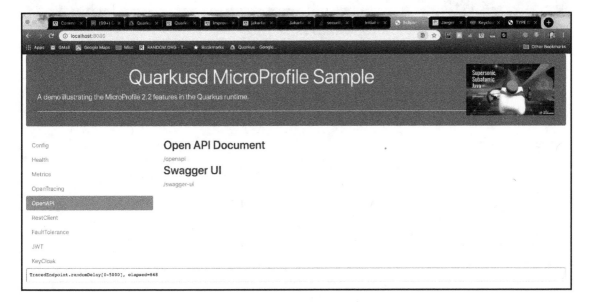

The first link generates an OpenAPI document, a YAML file that contains descriptions for all endpoints in the application. This can be fed into other programs or applications capable of consuming the OpenAPI format. The second link is an example of such an application, the Swagger UI. Opening that link will bring up a new window similar to the following:

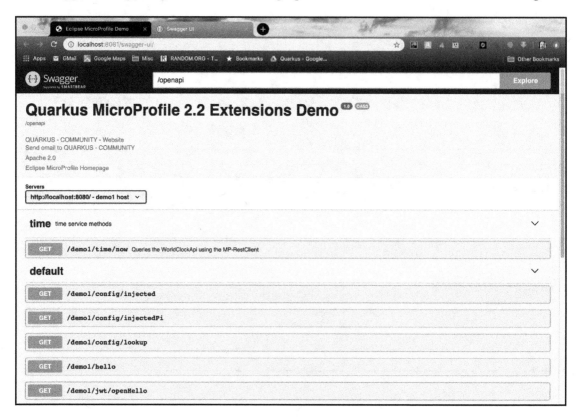

There are three sections in this view of the sample application. The first section is information that was specified on the JAX-RS application bean via the OpenAPI annotations, as shown in this code fragment:

```
@ApplicationPath("/demo1")
@LoginConfig(authMethod = "MP-JWT", realmName = "quarkus-quickstart")
@OpenAPIDefinition(
    info = @Info(
        title = "Quarkus MicroProfile 2.2 Extensions Demo",
        version = "1.0",
        contact = @Contact(
            name = "QUARKUS - COMMUNITY",
            url = "https://quarkus.io/community/",
            email = "quarkus-dev+subscribe@googlegroups.com"),
```

```
        license = @License(
            name = "Apache 2.0",
            url = "http://www.apache.org/licenses/LICENSE-2.0.html")
    ),
    servers = {
        @Server(url = "http://localhost:8080/", description = "demo1
host"),
        @Server(url = "http://localhost:8081/", description = "demo2 host")
    },
    externalDocs = @ExternalDocumentation(url="http://microprofile.io",
description =
    "Eclipse MicroProfile Homepage")
)
public class DemoRestApplication extends Application {
...
```

Comparing this information to that shown in the Swagger UI shows that all of the information from the @OpenAPIDefinition annotation has been incorporated into the UI top section. The next section of the Swagger UI with the time and default subheadings corresponds to the operation information taken from the application REST endpoint. The default section corresponds to endpoints that did not include any OpenAPI specification annotations. There is a default behavior to create an OpenAPI endpoint definition for any JAX-RS endpoint found in the application.

The time section corresponds to the following io.packt.sample.restclient.TimeService endpoint code fragment that has included the @Tag, @ExternalDocumentation, and @Operation MP-OpenAPI annotations:

```
@GET
@Path("/now")
@Produces(MediaType.APPLICATION_JSON)
@Tag(name = "time", description = "time service methods")
@ExternalDocumentation(description = "Basic World Clock API Home.",
    url = "http://worldclockapi.com/")
@Operation(summary = "Queries the WorldClockApi using the MP-RestClient",
    description = "Uses the WorldClockApi type proxy injected by the
    MP-RestClient to access the worldclockapi.com service")
public Now utc() {
    return clockApi.utc();
}
```

If you expand the first operation under the **time** section, you will obtain a view like this:

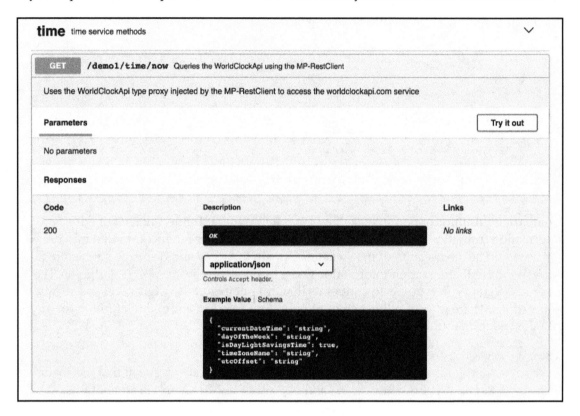

You can see that the @Tag has defined the **time** section and its description, and the @Operation annotation has augmented the operation summary and description sections. This shows how you can provide more information to consumers of your endpoints using the MP-OAPI annotations and OpenAPI aware apps like the Swagger UI.

# The KeyCloak tab

We'll skip to the **KeyCloak** tab next because the **RestClient** and **JWT** tabs include secured calls that require a JWT to access the endpoints. When you access the **KeyCloak** tab for the first time, it should look like the following:

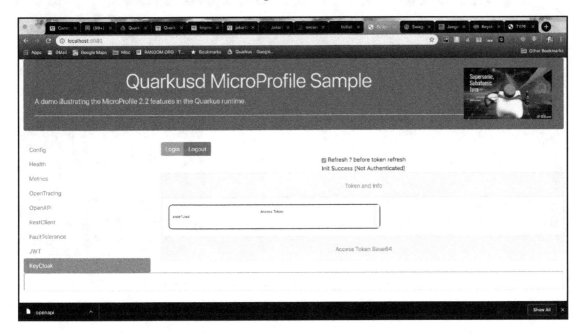

It will not show any token information, and the status line just below the **Refresh** checkbox should indicate (**Not Authenticated**). Click on the green **Login** button to bring up the following **Log In** screen:

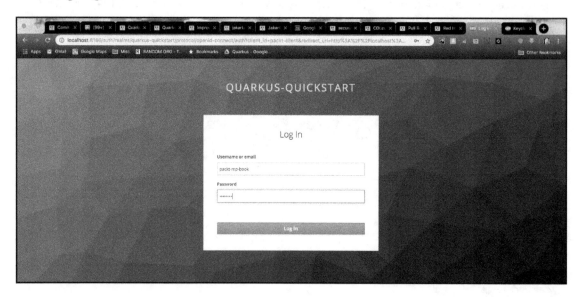

Enter the following for the **Username** and **Password** fields, respectively:

- `packt-mp-book`
- `password`

This username and password were created when we started KeyCloak in Docker and passed in the `packt-mp-realm.json` file to set up the realm that was created to support the example in this book.

You should be returned to the **KeyCloak** tab with a view that now includes **Access Token** information. The following screenshot contains a blow-up of the information obtained and decoded by the KeyCloak JavaScript library used by the application when I ran through the login process:

```
                                        Access Token
{
    "jti": "412ea590-5fe9-4411-85fb-76ecb7f45e7c",
    "exp": 1560809218,
    "nbf": 0,
    "iat": 1560808918,
    "iss": "http://localhost:8180/auth/realms/quarkus-quickstart",
    "aud": "account",
    "sub": "171e82ec-5a5d-446c-8d17-5ddec9116882",
    "typ": "Bearer",
    "azp": "packt-client",
    "nonce": "a54dc25d-472c-48db-a731-600058895ac3",
    "auth_time": 1560808918,
    "session_state": "b7258f3b-573b-405d-bf86-499bc0086f07",
    "acr": "1",
    "allowed-origins": [
        "http://localhost:8080"
    ],
    "realm_access": {
        "roles": [
            "PacktMPUser",
            "WorldClockSubscriber",
            "offline_access",
            "uma_authorization",
            "user"
        ]
    },
    "resource_access": {
        "packt-client": {
            "roles": [
                "MPJWTCompatible"
            ]
        },
        "account": {
            "roles": [
                "manage-account",
                "manage-account-links",
                "view-profile"
            ]
        }
    },
    "scope": "openid email profile",
    "upn": "packt-mp-book",
    "zoneinfo": "PST",
    "email_verified": false,
    "name": "Packt MpBook",
    "groups": [
        "PacktMPUser",
        "WorldClockSubscriber",
        "offline_access",
        "uma_authorization",
        "user"
```

This is the JSON content of the MP-JWT compatible token that was generated by the login action. This token will expire in 300 seconds, but the web app automatically refreshes it with the KeyCloak server as long as the **Refresh** checkbox is selected. There are a few claims of note that the sample application makes use of: the `zoneinfo=PST`, `upn=packt-mp-book`, and `groups=["PacktMPUser", ...]` claims.

The `zoneinfo` claim value is used in one of the secured `RestClient` calls, the `upn` claim is used in a few secured calls to identify the caller, and the groups claim provides the roles that have been assigned to the user and will determine which endpoints secured with the JAX-RS `@RolesAllowed("...")` annotations will be accessed using the JWT. We'll look at these in more detail in the following sections with secured endpoints.

Now that we can access the secured endpoints, let's go to the **JWT** tab.

# The JWT tab

After clicking on the **JWT** tab, you should see a view similar to the following with two endpoint links:

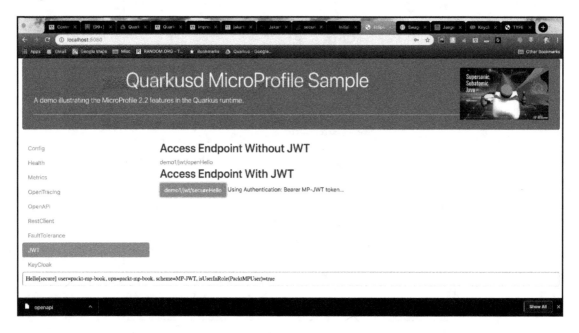

The first link makes a request to an unsecured endpoint that will print the name from the JWT along with the `upn` claim if it exists.

However, since the web frontend is not providing a JWT for this request, the following will be displayed in the output section:

```
Hello[open] user=anonymous, upn=no-upn
```

Clicking on the second link accesses a secured version of the endpoint that has this code fragment:

```
public class JwtEndpoint {
    @Inject
    private JsonWebToken jwt;
    @Inject
    @Claim(standard = Claims.raw_token)
    private ClaimValue<String> jwtString;
    @Inject
    @Claim(standard = Claims.upn)
    private ClaimValue<String> upn;
    @Context
    private SecurityContext context;
...
    @GET
    @Path("/secureHello")
    @Produces(MediaType.TEXT_PLAIN)
    @RolesAllowed("user") // 1
    public String secureHello() {
        String user = jwt == null ? "anonymous" : jwt.getName(); // 2
        String scheme = context.getAuthenticationScheme(); // 3
        boolean isUserInRole = context.isUserInRole("PacktMPUser"); // 4
        return String.format("Hello[secure] user=%s, upn=%s, scheme=%s,
        isUserInRole(PacktMPUser)=%s", user, upn.getValue(),
        scheme, isUserInRole);
    }
```

Let's discuss the important lines:

1. The `@RolesAllowed("user")` annotation indicates that the endpoint is secured and that the caller needs the user role. The JWT groups claim we saw earlier had this role.
2. The user is taken from the JWT via the getName() method. As explained in the MP-JWT chapter, this maps to the upn claim in the JWT.
3. The current security authentication scheme is obtained from the injected SecurityContext.
4. A programmatic security check of whether the caller has the PacktMPUser role is made. The check will return true as the JWT groups claim we saw earlier had this role.

This information is combined into a string that is the return value of the `secureHello` method. Clicking on the **demo1/jwt/secureHello** link button produces the following output string in the response area:

```
Hello[secure] user=packt-mp-book, upn=packt-mp-book, scheme=MP-JWT,
isUserInRole(PacktMPUser)=true
```

By using the combination of `@RolesAllowed` annotations and integration with the MP-JWT feature, we can see how we can both secure access to our microservice endpoints as well as introduce application behaviors based on content in the authenticated JWT. Next, let's return to the **RestClient** tab.

## The RestClient tab

The **RestClient** tab contains three links, as shown in this view:

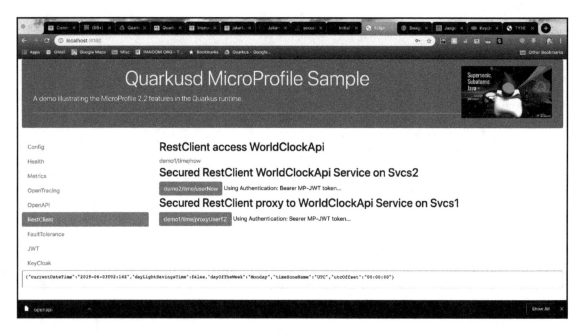

The links correspond to endpoints that make use of an external world clock public endpoint that returns information about the current time when accessed. The following MP-RC interface has been created to encapsulate the external endpoint:

```
@RegisterRestClient(baseUri = WorldClockApi.BASE_URL)
public interface WorldClockApi {
    static final String BASE_URL = "http://worldclockapi.com/api/json";
```

```
@GET
@Path("/utc/now")
@Produces(MediaType.APPLICATION_JSON)
Now utc();

@GET
@Path("{tz}/now")
@Produces(MediaType.APPLICATION_JSON)
Now tz(@PathParam("tz") String tz);
}
```

The first link accesses the `io.packt.sample.restclient.TimeService#utc()` method in the `svcs1` image that makes use of this `WorldClockApi` interface to obtain the current time in UTC without any use of a JWT. Hitting the first link will produce a string like the following:

```
{"currentDateTime":"2019-06-03T02:58Z","dayLightSavingsTime":false,"dayOfTh
eWeek":"Monday","timeZoneName":"UTC","utcOffset":"00:00:00"}
```

The second link accesses the `io.packt.sample.secure.TimeService#userNow()` method in the `svcs2` image. This call entails several pieces, so here is a sequence diagram illustrating the interaction between endpoints involved in the call:

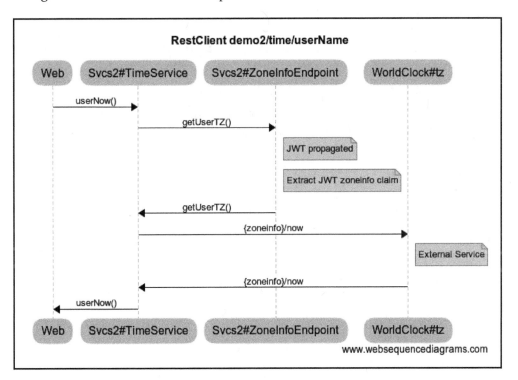

Let's see how this works:

- When the **Web** frontend calls the `userNow()` endpoint on `Svcs2#TimeService`, it includes the current JWT token even though the `TimeService` endpoint is not secured. This is because that endpoint will end up calling a secured endpoint to extract `zoneinfo` for the caller. The **Web** frontend properties that declare that the JWT authorization header should be propagated in calls are shown in the *Web MP-RC configuration*.
- The `Svcs2#TimeService#userNow()` endpoint method code is shown in `Svcs2:TimeService`. It uses an MP-RC interface defined later in `Svcs2:UserTimeZoneService MP-RC Interface`. This MP-RC interface uses the `@RegisterClientHeaders` annotation to propagate all of the incoming client request headers. `Svcs2#TimeService#userNow()` calls to the `Svcs2#ZoneInfoEndpoint#getSubscriberZoneInfo()` method to determine the caller's time zone.
- The `Svcs2#ZoneInfoEndpoint#getSubscriberZoneInfo()` method is shown in `Svcs2:ZoneInfoEndpoint`. This code injects the `zoneinfo` claim from the caller JWT and returns that from the `getSubscriberZoneInfo()` method, which is secured with `@RolesAllowed("WorldClockSubscriber")`. `WorldClockSubscriber` is a role we saw in the JWT `groups` claim.
- The `Svcs2#TimeService#userNow()` method uses `zoneinfo` to request the current time in that time zone by using the WorldClockApi MP-RC interface, passing in `zoneinfo` as the `tz` parameter.

So, now, click on the second link button, and you should see a string like the following displayed in the result output section:

```
{"currentDateTime":"2019-06-02T21:39-07:00","dayLightSavingsTime":false,"da
yOfTheWeek":"Sunday","timeZoneName":"Pacific Standard
Time","utcOffset":"-07:00:00"}
```

This time, the `currentDateTime` value is displayed in the PST time zone and the `timeZoneName` matches that.

The `Svcs2:UserTimeZoneService` MP-RC interface is as follows:

```
// svcs2/io.packt.sample.secure.UserTimeZoneService
@RegisterRestClient(baseUri = "http://localhost:8081/demo2/secure")
@RegisterClientHeaders
public interface UserTimeZoneService {
 @GET
 @Path("/userTZ")
 @Produces(MediaType.TEXT_PLAIN)
 String getUserTZ();
}
```

The `Svcs2:TimeService` endpoint is as follows:

```
// svcs2/io.packt.sample.secure.TimeService
@Path("/time")
@ApplicationScoped
public class
TimeService {
 @Inject
 @RestClient
 WorldClockApi clockApi;
 @Inject
 @RestClient
 UserTimeZoneService userTimeZone;

 @GET
 @Path("/userNow")
 @Produces(MediaType.APPLICATION_JSON)
 public Now userNow() {
 String tz = userTimeZone.getUserTZ();
 Now userTime = clockApi.tz(tz);
 System.out.printf("TimeService.userNow: %s\n", userTime);
 return userTime;
 }
}
```

The `Svcs2:ZoneInfoEndpoint` endpoint is as follows:

```
// svcs2/io.packt.sample.secure.ZoneInfoEndpoint
@Path("/protected")
@RequestScoped
public class ZoneInfoEndpoint {

 @Inject
 @Claim("zoneinfo")
 private String zoneinfo;
 @Inject
```

```
JsonWebToken jwt;

@GET
@Path("/userTZ")
@RolesAllowed("WorldClockSubscriber")
@Produces(MediaType.TEXT_PLAIN)
@Timed
public String getSubscriberZoneInfo() {
System.out.printf("Zoneinfo for %s: %s\n", jwt.getName(), zoneinfo);
return zoneinfo;
}
}
```

The Web MP-RC configuration is shown as follows:

```
# This overrides the WorldClockApi baseUri.
io.packt.sample.restclient.WorldClockApi/mp-rest/url=http://worldclockapi.c
om/api/json
# Propagate Authentication and OpenTracing headers
org.eclipse.microprofile.rest.client.propagateHeaders=Authorization,X-B3-
TraceId,X-B3-ParentSpanId,X-B3-SpanId,X-B3-Sampled
```

The `io.packt.sample.restclient.WorldClockApi/mp-rest/url` property sets the location of the `WorldClockApi` MP-RC endpoint to the public URL for the service. The `org.eclipse.microprofile.rest.client.propagateHeaders` property tells the MP-RC feature to automatically propagate any of the indicated incoming headers with the outgoing calls. This allows the headers that impact the MP-JWT and MP-OT features to be automatically propagated so that endpoints in the target containers of the outgoing calls will behave as expected even though the calls involve multiple MicroProfile containers in separate processes.

We have now looked at each of the MicroProfile features used in the sample application and have a better understanding of how we can build up a MicroProfile-based application using microservices and external services to create an application.

# Summary

This chapter has walked us through a sample service mesh composed of a web application, two microservice images using MP features in a new Quarkus implementation, an external web service, and two Docker-based services. This showed the interplay between the various MP features and external services you will find in cloud environments, along with integration with web services external to the local mesh environment. This should give you a feeling of the steps involved when composing microservices using the MicroProfile APIs and implementations.

In the next chapter, we will take a look at MicroProfile specifications that are under development to have an idea of what directions are being explored. While these specifications are currently outside of the MicroProfile core feature set, they are candidates for future inclusion, and looking at them will give us an idea of where MicroProfile may be headed.

# Questions

1. Do the MP-Config settings affect application code, MP feature code, or both?
2. Were you able to update `health.pathToMonitor` to a valid path and see an updated health status reply?
3. What does the `Svcs2` health status link (`http://localhost:8082/health`) on the **Health** tab show as its output? If you stop the KeyCloak Docker image and click on the link again, does the output change?
4. What happens if you select the `MetricController.timed-request` link (`http://localhost:8080/metrics/application/io.packt.sample.metric.MetricController.timed-request`) in the **Metrics** tab without first hitting the `Timed` endpoint link (`http://localhost:8080/demo1/metric/timed`) at least once?
5. Go to the **RestClient** tab and hit the link, making sure you have a valid JWT. Next, go to the **OpenTracing** tab and open the Jaeger UI, and pull up the current traces by clicking the **Find Traces** button. You should see a `QuarkusMPDemo: GET:io.packt.sample.restclient.TimeService.proxyUserTZ` trace. Click that and inspect the calls. Based on these calls, what is the difference between the second and third links on the **RestClient** page?

6. The Swagger UI allows us to access the endpoints from within the UI. Try accessing the `/demo1/time/now` endpoint using the Swagger UI. Are there differences relative to the Web UI of the sample application?

7. What happens if you log out on the **KeyCloak** tab and then try to access a secured endpoint or try to access a secured endpoint without logging into KeyCloak?

8. The **KeyCloak** tab has an **Access Base64 Token** section. What is displayed there when you are logged into KeyCloak? Is there anything you can do with that content?

# Further reading

Going over the code, trying changes, and then interacting with the updated code is a good way to understand more of the details behind the sample services. The Quarkus MicroProfile implementation supports live reload features that allow you to make changes without having to rebuild. For more information on this topic, see Maven Tooling (`https:/ /quarkus.io/guides/maven-tooling.html`) on the Quarkus site.

# Section 5: A Peek into the Future

**5**

This section covers existing projects that are outside the umbrella, such as candidate APIs, and discusses how MicroProfile fits into multi-cloud environments.

This section contains the following chapters:

- Chapter 9, *Reactive Programming and Future Developments*
- Chapter 10, *MicroProfile in Multi-Cloud Environments*

# Reactive Programming and Future Developments

Event-driven architectures have been around for a long time, and asynchronous method invocations, message-driven beans, event control logic, and so on are constructs that developers are familiar with. However, with the popularity and adoption of cloud resources and on-demand scalability, organizations have a renewed interest in reactive programming approaches that can exploit serverless and function as service-type environments. Eclipse MicroProfile also includes specifications related to reactive programming in projects that currently live outside the Eclipse MicroProfile umbrella/platform release.

In addition to these, there are also projects in the Eclipse MicroProfile sandbox that the community is currently discussing, implementing, and evaluating to decide whether or not they should be promoted to official MicroProfile projects. This chapter will help you learn about the current MicroProfile specifications related to reactive programming as well as give you a glimpse into what is already in motion and what is upcoming in relation to the projects that sit outside the umbrella/platform release and in the MicroProfile sandbox. The following topics will be covered in this chapter:

- An overview of what reactive messaging is
- An explanation of the reactive messaging architecture within Eclipse MicroProfile
- A description of the Eclipse MicroProfile specifications related to reactive programming
- Examples of how to use the reactive message specification of Eclipse MicroProfile
- An overview of MicroProfile projects/specifications that sit outside the umbrella or platform release
- A description of projects that sit within the Eclipse MicroProfile sandbox
- An insight into the current relationship between Eclipse MicroProfile and Jakarta EE and an analysis of their possible futures

# Reactive programming work in Eclipse MicroProfile

At the time of writing, the reactive-related specifications that are part of Eclipse MicroProfile are Reactive Streams Operators, Reactive Messaging, and Context Propagation. Reactive work within the MicroProfile community continues to evolve, and new specifications may surface in the future as well as newer releases of existing reactive-related ones.

## An overview of Reactive Messaging

The `Reactive Manifesto` defines the characteristics of reactive systems to including an asynchronous messaging core that is used to build elastic, resilient systems. This is typically illustrated via a diagram such as the following:

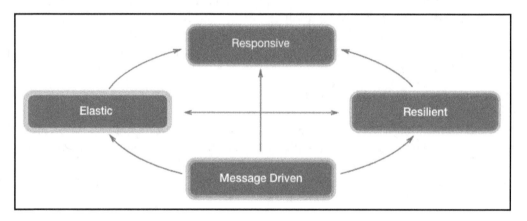

The idea is that interaction via asynchronous messages promotes resilience, elasticity, and, in turn, responsiveness.

The **MicroProfile Reactive Messaging (MP-RM)** specification aims to enable microservice-based applications with the characteristics of reactive systems via event-driven microservices. The specification focuses on versatility and is suitable for building different types of architecture and applications.

Asynchronous interactions with different services and resources can be implemented using reactive messaging. Typically, asynchronous database drivers can be used in conjunction with reactive messaging to read and write into a data store in a non-blocking and asynchronous manner.

When building microservices, **Command Query Responsibility Segregation (CQRS)** and event-sourcing patterns provide an answer to data sharing between microservices (`https:/ /martinfowler.com/bliki/CQRS.html`). Reactive messaging can also be used as the foundation for CQRS and the event-sourcing mechanism, as these patterns embrace message-passing as a core communication pattern.

## MicroProfile reactive messaging architecture

An application using reactive messaging is composed of CDI beans that consume, produce, and process messages. The messages can be internal to the application, or can be sent and received via external message brokers, as illustrated in the following diagram:

This figure shows a Kafka topic publishing messages to a first bean, which does some processing and publishes it to a second bean, which does its own processing/filtering, and finally publishes the message as an AMQP topic.

As we will see when we look into MP-RM examples, application beans contain methods annotated with `@Incoming` and/or `@Outgoing` annotations. A method with an `@Incoming` annotation consumes messages from a channel. A method with an `@Outgoing` annotation publishes messages to a channel. A method with both `@Incoming` and `@Outgoing` annotations is a message processor; it consumes messages from a channel, does some transformation on them, and publishes messages to another channel.

The architecture makes use of the following concepts:

- **Channels**: An opaque and unique name indicating which source or destination of messages is used. There are two types of channel:
    - Internal channels are local to the application. They allow the implementation of multi-step processing where several beans from the same application form a processing chain.
    - External channels are connected to remote brokers or various message transport layers, such as Apache Kafka, or to an AMQP broker. These channels are managed by connectors.

- **Messages**: A logical envelope wrapping a payload. A message is sent to a specific channel and, when received and processed successfully, is acknowledged.
- **Connectors**: These are extensions managing communication with a specific transport technology. They are responsible for mapping a specific channel to a remote sink or source of messages. This mapping is configured in the application configuration.
- **Reactive Streams**: A potentially infinite stream with operators that can filter and transform the stream content. The back pressure mechanism of reactive streams means that a publisher will not send data to a subscriber unless there are outstanding subscriber requests. This implies that the data flow along the stream is enabled by the first request for data received by the publisher. MP-RM depends on the JDK 6-compatible `org.reactivestreams` Reactive Stream API, which provides `Publisher`, `Subscriber`, `Subscription`, and `Processor` interfaces. For more information, you can check this link: `https://www.reactive-streams.org/`.
- **Message stream operators**: An API for manipulating reactive streams, providing operators such as `map`, `filter`, and `flatMap`, in a similar fashion to the `java.util.stream` API introduced in Java 8. It also provides an SPI for implementing and providing custom reactive stream engines, allowing application developers to use whichever engine they see fit.

## Message shapes

The MP-RM specification defines a number of supported signature types that beans can use to define publish and subscriber behaviors. These signatures depend on a few key types that are outlined in the following list:

- `org.reactivestreams.Publisher`: A Reactive Streams `Publisher<T>` is a provider of a potentially unlimited number of sequenced elements, publishing them according to the demand received from its link subscriber(s).
- `org.reactivestreams.Subscriber`: A Reactive Stream `Subscriber<T>` interface that is used to signal demand to `Publisher`. It provides events for subscription information, zero or more data events, and error and completion events.
- `org.reactivestreams.Processor`: This Reactive Stream `Processor<T,R>` interface simply extends both `Subscriber<T>` and `Publisher<R>`.

- `org.eclipse.microprofile.reactive.streams.operators.PublisherBu`
  `ilder`: The MP Reactive Streams Operators `PublisherBuilder` interface allows
  you to build up a Reactive Streams `Publisher` from various sources and apply
  operations to transform/filter ultimately published messages.

- `org.eclipse.microprofile.reactive.streams.operators.ProcessorBu`
  `ilder`: The MP Reactive Streams Operators `ProcessorBuilder` interface allows
  you to build up a Reactive Streams `Processor` from various sources and apply
  operations to transform/filter ultimately published messages.

- `org.eclipse.microprofile.reactive.streams.operators.SubscriberB`
  `uilder`: The MP Reactive Streams Operators `ProcessorBuilder`
  interface allows you to build up a Reactive Streams `Subscriber` from various
  sources and apply operations to transform/filter ultimately published messages.

- `java.util.concurrent.CompletionStage`: This JDK concurrent `util`
  package interface defines a stage of computation that is typically asynchronous,
  and computes an action or value. `CompletionStage` can be combined so that a
  graph of stages may be executed to produce the final result.

- `org.eclipse.microprofile.reactive.messaging.Message<T>`: An MP-
  RM interface that provides a wrapper around the payload of type `T` and an `ack`
  method to acknowledge receipt of the message.

With these types defined, we can look at the various types of method that produce data by
pushing messages onto outgoing channels that MP-RM supports. The publisher method
types of methods all have an `@Outgoing("channel-name")` annotation and support
signatures as follows:

- `Publisher<Message<T>> method()`
- `Publisher<T> method()`
- `PublisherBuilder<Message<T>> method()`
- `PublisherBuilder<T> method()`
- `T method()`
- `CompletionStage<T> method()`

Consumer methods all have an `@Incoming("channel-name")` annotation and support signatures as follows:

- `Subscriber<Message<T>> method()`
- `Subscriber<T> method()`
- `SubscriberBuilder<Message<T>>`
- `SubscriberBuilder<T>`
- `void method(Message<T> payload)`
- `void method(T payload)`
- `CompletionStage<?> method(Message<T> payload)`
- `CompletionStage<?> method(T payload)`

Methods that both consume and produce data are known as processors, and will have both an `@Incoming("channel-in")` and `@Outgoing("channel-out")` annotation. Supported signatures are as follows:

- `Processor<Message<I>, Message<O>> method()`
- `Processor<I, O> method();`
- `ProcessorBuilder<Message<I>, Message<O>>method()`
- `ProcessorBuilder<I, O> method();`
- `Publisher<Message<O>> method(Message<I> msg)`
- `Publisher<O> method(I payload)`
- `PublisherBuilder<Message<O>> method(Message<I> msg)`
- `PublisherBuilder<O> method(I payload)`
- `Message<O> method(Message<I> msg)`
- `O method(I payload)`
- `CompletionStage<Message<O>> method(Message<I> msg)`
- `CompletionStage<O> method(I payload)`
- `Publisher<Message<O>> method(Publisher<Message<I>> pub)`
- `PublisherBuilder<Message<O>> method(PublisherBuilder<Message<I>> pub)`
- `Publisher<O> method(Publisher<I> pub)`
- `PublisherBuilder<O> method(PublisherBuilder<I> pub)`

Now, we will look at some examples of using beans with these signatures to build up message processing chains.

# MicroProfile Reactive Streams operators

Reactive Streams requires more than just plumbing publishers to subscribers. Typically, a stream needs to be manipulated in some way, such as applying operations including `map`, `filter`, and `flatMap`. Neither Reactive Streams nor the JDK provide an API for performing these manipulations. Since users are not meant to implement Reactive Streams themselves, this means the only way to do these manipulations currently is to depend on a third-party library providing operators, such as Akka Streams, RxJava, or Reactor.

The MicroProfile Reactive Streams Operators API seeks to fill that gap so that MicroProfile application developers can manipulate Reactive Streams without bringing in a third-party dependency. By itself, this API is not useful to MicroProfile, but with the addition of other Reactive features, such as MicroProfile Reactive Messaging, it is essential.

# MicroProfile Context Propagation

This specification, which sits outside the MicroProfile umbrella of platform release, is still in the proposed or draft state. We will discuss this specification in more detail in the *MicroProfile Future Developments* section later in this chapter, but we would like to give you a high-level introduction here.

The MicroProfile Context Propagation specification introduces APIs for propagating contexts across units of work that are thread-agnostic. It makes it possible to propagate context that was traditionally associated with the current thread across various types of units of work, such as `CompletionStage`, `CompletableFuture`, `Function`, and `Runnable`, regardless of which particular thread ends up executing them.

# MicroProfile reactive messaging examples

In this section, we will cover some examples of using MP-RM to create CDI beans that produce and consume messages.

Let's say you want a CDI bean to act as a source of a `Message<String>` such that whenever its `publishMessage(String)` method is called, an MP-RM message is posted to some MP-RM channel. To do this, we need to define a connector that bridges between the CDI bean and the MP-RM layer. An example of an incoming message connector that does this is shown in the following code:

```
package io.pckt.reactive;

import javax.enterprise.context.ApplicationScoped;
```

```
import javax.inject.Inject;

import org.eclipse.microprofile.config.Config;
import org.eclipse.microprofile.reactive.messaging.Message;
import org.eclipse.microprofile.reactive.messaging.spi.Connector;
import
org.eclipse.microprofile.reactive.messaging.spi.IncomingConnectorFactory;
import
org.eclipse.microprofile.reactive.streams.operators.PublisherBuilder;
import
org.eclipse.microprofile.reactive.streams.operators.SubscriberBuilder;

@ApplicationScoped
@Connector(BeanConnector.CONNECTOR_NAME) (1)
public class BeanConnector implements IncomingConnectorFactory (2) {
    public static final String CONNECTOR_NAME = "cdibean";
    @Inject
    BeanSource beanSource; (3)

    public BeanConnector() {
        System.out.printf("BeanConnector.ctor\n");
    }

    @Override
    public PublisherBuilder<? extends Message> getPublisherBuilder(Config
    config) {
       System.out.printf("getPublisherBuilder, config=%s\n", config);
       return beanSource.source(); (4)
    }
}
```

1. The `@Connector` annotation defines this as an MP-RM connector and specifies the name of the connector.
2. A connector supports either an incoming or outgoing factory, or both. We will only implement the outgoing factory to create a message publisher.
3. The injected `BeanSource` is the CDI bean that transforms method invocation into outgoing messages.
4. We obtain the outgoing `PublisherBuilder` instance from the `BeanSource#source()` method. We will look at this code in the next example.

Now, the associated `BeanSource` is given in the following example code:

```
package io.packt.reactive;

import java.util.concurrent.CompletableFuture;
```

```
import javax.enterprise.context.ApplicationScoped;

import io.reactivex.processors.BehaviorProcessor;
import org.eclipse.microprofile.reactive.messaging.Message;
import
org.eclipse.microprofile.reactive.streams.operators.PublisherBuilder;
import org.eclipse.microprofile.reactive.streams.operators.ReactiveStreams;

@ApplicationScoped
public class BeanSource {
    CompletableFuture<Message<String>> future = new CompletableFuture<>();
    BehaviorProcessor<Message<String>> processor =
    BehaviorProcessor.create(); (1)

    public void publishMessage(String payload) (2){
        System.out.printf("publishMessage, payload=%s\n", payload);
        Message<String> msg = Message.of(payload); (3)
        processor.onNext(msg); (4)
    }
    public void done() {
        future.complete(Message.of("End of transmission"));
    }
    public PublisherBuilder<? extends Message> source() { (5)
        PublisherBuilder<? extends Message> publisherBuilder =
        ReactiveStreams.fromPublisher(processor);
        return publisherBuilder;
    }
}
```

Let's see how this works:

1. `BehaviorProcessor` is a Reactive Streams processor implementation that emits the most recent item it has observed and all subsequent observed items to each subscriber.

2. The `publishMessage(String)` method takes a method invocation

3. This then wraps the incoming payload in an MP-RM

4. This, in turn, passes the message to the `BehaviorProcessor` so it can pass the message to all subscribers of the channel that will be configured to use the connector.

So, how would this connector get mapped to an MP-RM channel? We need to configure this using the MP-Config properties defined by MP-RM. The pattern for setting an incoming channel connector is as follows:

```
mp.messaging.incoming.[channel-name].connector=[connector-name]
```

So, to map an `@Incoming("sink")` annotated consumer to use the `cdibean` connector, you would specify the following:

```
mp.messaging.incoming.sink.connector=cdibean
```

With this configuration, any invocation of the `BeanSource#publishMessage(String)` method would result in the method argument being sent to all subscribers of the `sink` channel.

Now, let's look at an example of a message producer bean method that generates a 100-second counter stream, as shown in the following example:

```
package io.packt.reactive;

import java.util.concurrent.atomic.AtomicInteger;
import java.util.function.Supplier;

import javax.enterprise.context.ApplicationScoped;

import org.eclipse.microprofile.reactive.messaging.Outgoing;
import
org.eclipse.microprofile.reactive.streams.operators.PublisherBuilder;
import org.eclipse.microprofile.reactive.streams.operators.ReactiveStreams;

@ApplicationScoped
public class CounterSource {
    @Outgoing("counter")  (1)
    public PublisherBuilder<Integer> nextCount() {
        final AtomicInteger count = new AtomicInteger(0);
        Supplier<Integer> counter = () -> {  (2)
            try {
                Thread.sleep(1000);
            } catch (Exception e) {
            }
            return count.incrementAndGet();
        };
        PublisherBuilder<Integer> publisherBuilder =
        ReactiveStreams.generate(counter).limit(100);  (3)
        return publisherBuilder;
    }
}
```

1. The `@Outgoing("counter")` annotation indicates that this is a publisher of messages and that the name of the channel is `counter`.

2. Here, we wrap a Java concurrency util, `Supplier`, in `PublisherBuilder` to create the stream of `Integer`.

3. The MP-RM `ReactiveStreams` utility interface is used to transform the integer stream into `PublisherBuild<Integer>` and then limits the number of messages to 100.

An example consumer bean that accepts both `counter` and `sink` channel producers shown previously is given in the following example:

```java
import java.util.ArrayList;
import java.util.List;

import javax.enterprise.context.ApplicationScoped;

import org.eclipse.microprofile.reactive.messaging.Acknowledgment;
import org.eclipse.microprofile.reactive.messaging.Incoming;

@ApplicationScoped
public class TestBean {
  static final List<String> COLLECTOR = new ArrayList<>();

  @Incoming("sink")
  @Acknowledgment(Acknowledgment.Strategy.PRE_PROCESSING)
  public void sink(String input) {
    System.out.printf("TestBean.incoming(sink), input=%s\n", input);
  }

  @Incoming("counter")
  @Acknowledgment(Acknowledgment.Strategy.PRE_PROCESSING)
  public void counted(Integer input) {
    System.out.printf("TestBean.incoming(counter), input=%s\n", input);
  }

}
```

Here, the `sink` and `counted` methods act as simple consumers that accept whatever messages are sent to the associated `@Incoming` channels and terminate the processing chain.

In the next section, we will look at projects that are currently in development as possible future MicroProfile specifications.

# MicroProfile future developments

As mentioned in Chapter 2, *Governance and Contributions*, new ideas brought to the Eclipse MicroProfile project are first tried in the MicroProfile sandbox following an implementation-first approach to innovation. The sandbox exercise gives the opportunity for the implementor and the community to discuss, analyze, and evaluate how this new idea fits in with the MicroProfile project. If, at the end of the sandbox exercise, the community deems that this new idea is worth adding to the project, a specific MicroProfile sub-project is created for it. The sub-project must issue at least one release before it can be considered for addition to a MicroProfile umbrella/platform release. At a very high-level, this is the process that new ideas and future developments follow under the MicroProfile project.

In the next sections, we will discuss two types of projects those globally that are currently MicroProfile sub-projects that presebtly sit outside the MicroProfile umbrella/platform release (think of these as projects that have already graduated out of the MicroProfile sandbox), and the ones that are still in the MicroProfile sandbox. Lastly, we will discuss the current relationship between Eclipse MicroProfile and Jakarta EE and how their roadmaps may or may not meet.

# Projects outside the umbrella

In this section, we will cover projects that sit outside the Eclipse MicroProfile umbrella release, at the time of writing, of course. These are as follows:

- Reactive Streams Operators
- Reactive Messaging
- Long Running Actions
- Context Propagation
- GraphQL

Reactive Streams Operators and Reactive Messaging projects were already discussed in the previous sections of this chapter, so in this section we will cover only Long Running Actions, Context Propagation, and GraphQL.

# Long Running Actions

In a loosely-coupled service environment, the motivation behind the **Long Running Actions** (**LRA**) specification is to provide consistent outcomes by business processes comprised of calls to many microservices without the need to lock data. One way to think about LRA is as *transactions for microservices*. Examples of situations when you need LRA include the following:

- Ordering a book online will require the retirement of a book from the inventory, the processing of a payment, and finally shipping of the book. All these tasks need to happen atomically, in other words, they need to be processed all together, in that, if any of the tasks fail, then all tasks must be undone.
- Making a flight reservation will require the removal of a seat from the airplane's list of available seats, the selection and assignment of a specific seat to the traveler, processing the payment, and the creation of a record locator. Again, all these tasks have to happen within the same long running action.

Not only do the preceding examples have to happen atomically, but they also have to generate a result where the data is consistent, even if any of their intermediate steps failed.

The current proposed solution for MicroProfile LRA has taken its inspiration from the *OASIS Web Services Composite Application Framework Technical Committee* (`https://www.oasis-open.org/committees/tc_home.php?wg_abbrev=ws-caf`), namely, the *Web Services Long Running Action transaction model* (`https://www.oasis-open.org/committees/document.php?document_id=12794`), but has been updated to be more suited for use in microservice-based architectures.

> For further information on the MicroProfile LRA specification, refer to `https://github.com/eclipse/microprofile-lra/blob/master/spec/src/main/asciidoc/microprofile-lra-spec.adoc`.

The MicroProfile Long Running Actions specification model includes three main entities: compensators, a logical coordinator, and a client. A client can explicitly start a new LRA in two different ways:

- Via an annotation, or
- Via an API call

Either one creates a new LRA. If a service does something that may need to be later undone, then the client needs to register a compensator with the LRA. If the client chooses to close or cancel the LRA, the compensator will undo the work the service performed within the scope of the LRA or compensate for any uncompleted work.

The following are globally some of the main LRA annotations:

- `@LRA` controls the life cycle of an LRA.
- `@Compensate` indicates that the method should be invoked if the LRA is canceled.
- `@Complete` indicates that the method should be invoked if the LRA is closed.
- `@Forget` indicates that the method may release any resources that were allocated for this LRA.
- `@Leave` indicates that this class is no longer interested in this LRA.
- `@Status` reports the status when the annotated method is invoked.

You can use these annotations with JAX-RS and non-JAX-RS methods. In addition, this specification supports asynchronous and reactive features of JAX-RS, LRA nesting, and timeouts. Finally, it is worth mentioning that the LRA specification ensures atomicity and eventual consistency by placing certain requirements on the entities that participate in the protocol. As a MicroProfile project, the MicroProfile LRA specification, at the time of writing, is in a proposed or draft state.

# Context Propagation

The goal of the MicroProfile Context Propagation specification is to propagate context across units of work that are thread-agnostic. In a reactive model, the execution of logic is split into units of work that are chained together to assemble a reactive pipeline. Each unit of work executes within a context, which is often unpredictable and depends on the particular reactive engine being used. Some units might run with the context of a thread awaiting completion, or the context of a previous unit that completed and triggered the dependent unit, or with no context at all. The MicroProfile Context Propagation specification makes it possible for thread context propagation to easily be done in a type-safe manner, keeping boilerplate code to a minimum and allowing for thread context propagation to be done automatically whenever possible.

For more information about the MicroProfile Context Propagation specification, please refer to https://github.com/eclipse/microprofile-context-propagation.

The MicroProfile Context Propagation specification has two implementations:

- ManagedExecutor: This provides methods for obtaining managed instances of CompletableFuture that are backed by the managed executor as the default asynchronous execution facility and the default mechanism for defining thread context propagation. The MicroProfile ManagedExecutor builder also implements the Java SE java.util.concurrent.ExecutorService interface, using managed threads when asynchronous invocation is required.
- ThreadContext: This provides methods for individually contextualizing units of work such as CompletionStage, CompletionFuture, Runnable, Function, and Supplier, without tying them to a particular thread execution model and giving the user fine-grained control over the capture and propagation of thread context by remaining thread execution-agnostic.

ManagedExecutor and ThreadContext are instantiated via their builder() APIs, which allows the user to specify a variety of parameter options that can also be configured using Eclipse MicroProfile Config mechanisms. An example of how to use the ManagedExecutor builder is as follows:

```
ManagedExecutor executor = ManagedExecutor.builder()
  .propagated(ThreadContext.APPLICATION)
  .cleared(ThreadContext.ALL_REMAINING)
  .maxAsync(5)
  .build();
```

An example of how to use the ThreadContext builder is as follows:

```
ThreadContext threadContext = ThreadContext.builder()
  .propagated(ThreadContext.APPLICATION, ThreadContext.CDI)
  .cleared(ThreadContext.ALL_REMAINING)
  .build();
```

Lastly, a convenient mechanism for sharing instances across an application is the definition of CDI producers as application scope, combined with injection.

# GraphQL

GraphQL is an open source data query and manipulation language for APIs, and a runtime for fulfilling queries with existing data. It interprets strings from the client and returns data in an understandable, predictable, and predefined manner. GraphQL is an alternative to REST, though not necessarily a replacement. The goal of the MicroProfile GraphQL specification is to provide a set of APIs to enable users to quickly develop portable GraphQL-based applications in Java. As a MicroProfile project, the MicroProfile GraphQL specification is currently, at the time of writing, in a proposed or draft state.

 GraphQL is based on a Facebook specification. For more information on this, please refer to `https://graphql.github.io/graphql-spec`. A more general overview of GraphQL can be found on `https://graphql.org/`.

GraphQL and REST have many similarities and are both widely used in modern microservice-based applications.

## Differences between GraphQL and REST

Here are the main differentiating features of GraphQL when compared to REST:

- **Schema-driven**: The schema acts as a contract between the server and its clients.
- **Single HTTP endpoint**: A single endpoint and access to data and operations are achieved through the query language.
- **Flexible data retrieval**: Enables the client to select data in the response with a fine level of granularity, thereby avoiding over- or under-fetching data.
- **Reduction of server requests**: The language allows the client to aggregate the expected data into a single request.
- **Easier version management**: Enables the creation of new data while deprecating old ones.
- **Partial results**: A result is made up of data and errors. Clients are responsible for processing the partial results.
- **Low coupling with HTTP**: Unlike REST, GraphQL does not try to make the most of HTTP semantics. For example, queries can be made using `GET` or `POST` requests. The HTTP result code does not reflect the GraphQL response.

- **Challenging authorization handling**: An appropriate data access authorization policy must be defined and implemented to counter the extreme flexibility of the query language.
- **Challenging API management**: GraphQL API has a single entry point. It may be necessary to analyze the client request data to ensure that it conforms to established policies.

### GraphQL and databases

GraphQL is not a database technology. Instead, it is a data query and manipulation tool for APIs and is agnostic to any database or storage technologies. However, it can be used in front of any backend and is capable of aggregating data from multiple backend data sources with a single API.

# Projects in the sandbox

The MicroProfile Project sandbox is where the community can come up with ideas by trying out an implementation of features and capabilities to elicit feedback, discussion, and evaluation from members within the community with the goal of deciding whether or not the idea should become a new API/specification for the MicroProfile project.

The MicroProfile sandbox is located at `https://github.com/eclipse/microprofile-sandbox`.

Past project proposals that graduated from the sandbox into official MicroProfile projects were GraphQL and Reactive Streams Operators. At the time of writing, there is only one proposal project in the sandbox, Boost.

# MicroProfile Boost

At the time of writing, the MicroProfile Boost is under community evaluation in the MicroProfile sandbox. Boost is a Maven plugin that enhances builds for your MicroProfile applications.

For more information on Boost, go to `https://github.com/eclipse/microprofile-sandbox/tree/master/proposals/boost`.

Boost defines Maven dependencies, known as **boosters**, for MicroProfile APIs, for example `mpConfig` for MicroProfile Config, as well as for Java EE APIs. In addition, it defines dependencies for the runtimes that implement the different MicroProfile APIs, for example `openliberty`. One more Boost-defined maven dependency specified as a BOM (Bill-of-Material) indicates the version of the MicroProfile umbrella project to use for the maven build with respect to the MicroProfile APIs. The BOM contents are managed by the plugin. As a user of Boost, you include these dependencies in your `pom.xml` file to ease the build process of your MicroProfile application.

# Eclipse MicroProfile and Jakarta EE

What is the relationship between the Eclipse Jakarta Enterprise Java project and the Eclipse MicroProfile project? Short answer: it remains to be seen. Long answer: let's begin.

The Eclipse MicroProfile project was initiated to address a lack of progress in the Java EE specifications under the **Java Community Process (JCP)**.

> For more information on the Java Community Process, please visit
> `https://jcp.org/en/home/index`.

It has been over two years since the MicroProfile project moved to the Eclipse Foundation. Approximately one year later, Oracle announced its intention to move Java EE over to the Eclipse Foundation and rename it Jakarta EE. The move to Jakarta has been a long drawn-out process that is still not completely finalized. The negotiations between Oracle and the Eclipse Foundation resulted in a requirement that future versions of the Jakarta EE specifications that are updated should require that the associated `javax.*` package names of APIs in the specification be changed to use a `jakarta.*` package.

In the Jakarta Platform development mailing list discussion of how this package migration should happen, it is clear that there is a desire by some Java EE developers that the Jakarta and MicroProfile projects should merge in some way. However, in MicroProfile hangout meetings where the topic has come up, there is a clear undercurrent of desire to maintain the MicroProfile project as an entity separate from Jakarta. There are suggestions that MicroProfile could be an incubator-type project that develops new specifications that are later promoted to Jakarta EE specifications as the need arises; the MicroProfile Configuration project started this conversion prior to Java EE moving from the JCP. So, while the configuration project continues to evolve under MicroProfile, it may still also undergo development under the Jakarta project.

Since the MicroProfile project depends on a few core Jakarta specifications, as these evolve, the MicroProfile project will likely update its dependencies on the updated specifications in a future MicroProfile platform version. MicroProfile community participants will be involved in updating those core specifications as they have a vested interest in their evolution.

So, while there almost certainly will be some interaction between the MicroProfile and Jakarta communities, the exact nature of that relationship from a formalized perspective is still to be determined. It is possible that the Jakarta and MicroProfile projects may share some procedural roots in the future, or they may simply continue as independent projects where MicroProfile is a client/consumer of Jakarta EE, and the MicroProfile project may look to promote projects to Jakarta EE as they are deemed to have matured and/or need longer-term stabilization under a Jakarta EE profile.

No matter how things end up, both projects can benefit from one another. The benefit that MicroProfile provides to Jakarta EE is the rapid innovation and proofing of new microservice APIs that could then be promoted to the Jakarta EE standards. Likewise, Jakarta EE can serve as a stable, reliable, standards-based platform where MicroProfile APIs can continue to be used. Customers also benefit from having two projects. Using terminology from the five stages of technology adoption, the innovators, early adopters, and those who want to get their hands on the leading edge of microservices specifications, can choose MicroProfile, while the late majority, laggards, and those who prefer established standards, can choose Jakarta EE.

# Summary

In this chapter, we learned about future developments in the MicroProfile specification with the Long Running Actions, Context Propagation, and GraphQL projects outside the umbrella release, and the Boost project that's still in the MicroProfile sandbox. In addition, you learned about reactive messaging concepts, the MicroProfile reactive messaging architecture, and how to implement reactive microservices using Eclipse MicroProfile reactive constructs via code examples. You also gained some knowledge of the background of each of these projects, their capabilities, annotations, and code examples when applicable, as well as their current state. Lastly, we presented the relationship between two similar but different projects: Eclipse MicroProfile and Jakarta EE, and discussed how their possible relationship could evolve in the future.

In the next chapter, we will learn about Eclipse MicroProfile in multi-cloud environments and deployments.

# Questions

1. If I have a source of messages, how do I integrate this into my MicroProfile applications?
2. Which of the existing MicroProfile specifications will MicroProfile Context Propagation best support?
3. What are the current MicroProfile specifications that support reactive programming?
4. What are the MicroProfile specifications that currently sit outside the umbrella/platform MicroProfile release?
5. What is the purpose of having a MicroProfile sandbox?
6. What are the projects that currently sit in the MicroProfile sandbox?
7. What is the current relationship between Eclipse MicroProfile and Jakarta EE?
8. What will the future relationship between Eclipse MicroProfile and Jakarta EE look like?

# Further reading

- For MicroProfile reactive messaging, the `http://reactivex.io/` site provides motivation, tutorials, language bindings, and more.
- A good starting point for GraphQL is the `https://graphql.org/` site, which provides more background on the motivation behind it, as well as many resources for exploring how to put it to use.

# 10
# Using MicroProfile in Multi-Cloud Environments

Microservices and microservices architectures are ideal development approaches for cloud and multi-cloud environments, including hybrid cloud deployments, where your application comprises on-premise logic as well as logic that runs in the cloud. Eclipse MicroProfile is a specification that optimizes Java for microservices architecture and thus provides constructs so that you can implement microservices in Java and the cloud. These topics will help you to understand why Eclipse MicroProfile is ideal for developing applications in hybrid and multi-cloud environments, and what you must take into consideration when using it in these types of deployments.

In this chapter, we will discuss the following topics:

- How Eclipse MicroProfile facilitates cloud-native application development
- How Eclipse MicroProfile relates to cloud-native and container-native application development
- The relationship between Eclipse MicroProfile and the 12-factor app
- How Eclipse MicroProfile can be used in serverless and **Function-as-a-Service (FaaS)** environments
- Eight steps to guide your journey to cloud-native applications and how Eclipse MicroProfile can help at each step
- Considerations when using Eclipse MicroProfile to develop applications that span across clouds
- When to run Eclipse MicroProfile on bare-metal machines versus **virtual machines (VMs)** versus containers
- What to consider when running Eclipse MicroProfile microservices in hybrid cloud applications

- What challenges to be aware of when running Eclipse MicroProfile OpenTracing in a multi-cloud deployment
- What to consider when using Eclipse MicroProfile in a service mesh

# Using Eclipse MicroProfile for cloud-native application development

What is a cloud-native application? Typically, a definition for **cloud-native** entails the following characteristics:

- Designed as loosely coupled services, such as microservices
- Loosely coupled services that interact via language-independent communication protocols, which allow microservices to be implemented in different programming languages and frameworks
- Lightweight containers that can scale up and down on-demand or via resource utilization metrics
- Managed through Agile DevOps processes, with each microservice of a cloud-native application going through an independent life cycle that's managed through an Agile process using **continuous integration/continuous delivery (CI/CD)** pipelines

However, Eclipse MicroProfile's goal is to optimize Java for microservice architectures, so does it make it suitable for cloud-native application development? What about container-native development? What is the relationship between microservices, cloud-native development, and container-native development? How do these differ or compare? Let's find out!

# Microservices versus cloud native versus container native

First, let's draw the differences between these three terms with respect to how an application is developed. As we discussed in Chapter 1, *Introduction to Eclipse MicroProfile*, an Enterprise Java microservice has the following features:

- It is a microservice written using the Java language.
- It can use any Java framework.
- It can use any Java API.

- It must be enterprise grade, which means it must have high reliability, availability, scalability, security, robustness, and performance.
- It must fulfill the characteristics of a microservice, all of which are listed at `https://martinfowler.com/microservices/`.

By its definition, a microservice does not prescribe specific details of the underlying platform on which it runs. The microservice definition is about the how, not the specific product or technology to use when writing a microservice. However, when we talk about an Enterprise Java microservice, the only functional requirements that are imposed are all, of course, related to the Java language. This implies that a microservice – or any Enterprise Java microservice – can run on any underlying platform that will support it, whether this is on bare-metal machines, virtualized ones, or in cloud or containerized environments. In fact, microservices and the microservices architecture started being implemented and deployed by organizations on bare-metal, virtualized, and cloud environments, even before containers were popularized.

Cloud native is a term that was first coined by Netflix around 2010, and its meaning has more to do with where and how an application, service, or microservice is developed in the cloud. *Born-on-the-cloud* is a term that's evoked by cloud native, but this is a simplistic way of looking at it. Cloud native encompasses technologies and methodologies on how to develop an application in the cloud. The **Cloud Native Computing Foundation** (CNCF) is part of the non-profit Linux Foundation and serves as the vendor-neutral home for many open source cloud native technologies. The CNCF defines cloud native as a set of technologies that permit organizations to run applications in the clouds, whether they are private, public, or hybrid. These technologies, which include microservices, service meshes, containers, APIs, immutable infrastructures, and so on, together with rigorous automation, facilitate systems that are loosely coupled, resilient, observable, and manageable, allow developers to make impactful changes with minimal effort.

So, cloud native is inclusive of technologies and techniques that permit the building and running of scalable applications at web scale. Some of these may be containers, automation, DevOps, microservices, API-driven development, and so on. But do you need containers to be cloud native? You can create cloud-native applications on virtualized and cloud environments without the need for containers. However, as the market is now realizing, to gain even more productivity, operational reliability, and flexibility, containers and container orchestration are great cloud-native technologies to use. This brings us to the question, *what is container native?*

Containers and microservices are examples of technologies and approaches that empower organizations to do cloud-native development. **Container-native** describes an application that has been written to take advantage of container technologies, such as Docker, Buildah, Podman, Kubernetes, and OpenShift. In other words, it's an application that has been developed and implemented for containers and its rich ecosystem of technologies.

In short, microservices that are developed using containers as their units of deployment provide one of the best approaches to developing highly distributed systems in the cloud and on-premises. Likewise, Eclipse MicroProfile provides one of the best approaches when it comes to developing microservices using Enterprise Java. But what about 12-factor applications? Can you use Eclipse MicroProfile to develop 12-factor applications?

# What about 12-factor applications?

Just like the microservices and microservices architecture definitions, a 12-factor app does not prescribe the underlying technologies, for example, the programming language, database, caches, and so on, or frameworks that should be used to implement them. The 12-factor app is a methodology that's used for implementing applications. These twelve factors are as follows:

- One codebase tracked in revision control, many deploys
- Explicitly declare and isolate dependencies
- Store config in the environment
- Treat backing services as attached resources
- Strictly separate build and run stages
- Execute the app as one or more stateless processes
- Export services via port binding
- Scale out via the process model
- Maximize robustness with fast startup and graceful shutdown
- Keep development, staging, and production as similar as possible
- Treat logs as event streams
- Run admin/management tasks as one-off processes

Implementing an application using this methodology helps us do the following:

- Minimize time and cost for new developers joining the project
- Offer portability between execution environments

- Easily deploy the application to cloud platforms
- Minimize the differences between development and production
- Scale it up without changes

 You can read all about the 12 factors at `https://12factor.net`.

The 12-factor app is a methodology that a developer can follow while designing and implementing microservices and applications, independent of the programming language or framework that's being used to implement them. The framework that a developer can use to implement microservices using the 12-factor app is Eclipse MicroProfile. The 12-factor app and Eclipse MicroProfile are not mutually exclusive but really complement each other.

But what about a methodology for designing and implementing applications that's not the 12-factor app? What about serverless and **Function-as-a-Service** (**FaaS**) technologies? How does Eclipse MicroProfile fit into these newer cloud-native technologies?

# What about serverless and FaaS?

Serverless and FaaS cloud-native technologies have been experiencing steady interest and growth in the market, as evidenced by offerings from all the major cloud providers, that is, AWS Lambda, Azure Functions, Oracle Functions, and Google Cloud Functions. In an era where organizations are increasingly using the cloud for development and production workloads, and compute and memory costs are operational expenses that need to be tracked and monitored, FaaS is attractive because it abstracts compute and memory management away from the user, who is then able to focus on developing business logic, thereby becoming a lot more productive than ever before.

With FaaS, developers don't need to set up VMs and memory, install software on them, or manage software versions, updates, and patches. This is all hidden away from the user in a FaaS, which typically charges per invocation and execution time. Developers can dedicate their time to writing just the logic that each call to a FaaS will execute. Each function should start up fast, be short-lived (no long-running logic should be executed in a FaaS), and do one task well, which is very similar to what a microservice does. Therefore, a microservice approach can be used for implementing functions for a FaaS.

Most –if not all – market FaaS offerings support Java. As such, developers can write the function bodies in one of the many implementations of Eclipse MicroProfile, which are all in Java. The ease of use and rich functionality of Eclipse MicroProfile, combined with the simplicity of a FaaS platform, can greatly improve the ability of developers to deliver value to the business faster. In addition, a technology such as Quarkus, which implements Eclipse MicroProfile, uses low amounts of memory, and has fast start up times, is an ideal runtime for a FaaS.

Now that we have discussed how Eclipse MicroProfile is well suited for cloud-native application development as well as serverless and FaaS environments, let's discuss how Eclipse MicroProfile can help organizations on the path to cloud-native application development.

# Cloud-native application development

There are two complementary aspects or components to cloud-native application development: application services and infrastructure services. Application services speed up the development of the business logic of a cloud-native application, and infrastructure services speed up its delivery and deployment. These two aspects are complementary and integral to cloud-native application development. You cannot have one without the other. They are essentially the yin and the yang of cloud-native application development, as depicted by the following diagram:

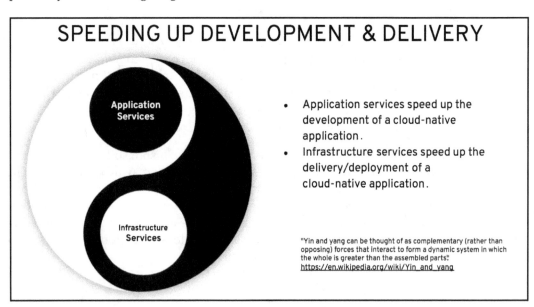

As we mentioned earlier in this chapter, cloud-native application development is an approach to building and running applications that takes full advantage of the cloud computing model, which is based on four key tenets:

- A service-based architecture (miniservices, microservices, SOA services, and so on)
- An API-driven approach for inter-service communication
- An underlying infrastructure that's based on containers
- DevOps processes

The following diagram depicts the four key tenets of cloud-native application development:

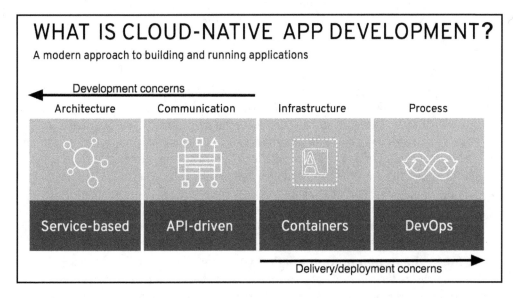

As shown in the previous diagram, the architecture and communication aspects are related to the development concerns of cloud-native applications, and the infrastructure and the process aspects are related to their delivery/deployment.

Organizations who are on their journey to adopting cloud-native application development can benefit from eight steps, as described by the e-Book titled *The path to cloud-native applications: 8 steps to guide your journey.*

To obtain the e-Book *The path to cloud-native applications: 8 steps to guide your journey,* please refer to https://www.redhat.com/en/resources/ path-to-cloud-native-applications-ebook.

Let's discuss how Eclipse MicroProfile can play a role in these eight steps:

1. **Evolve the DevOps culture and practices**: *"Take advantage of new technology, faster approaches, and tighter collaboration by embracing the principles and cultural values of DevOps and organizing your organization around those values."* Although this is an organizational and process-related step, Eclipse MicroProfile, as a specification for microservices, can be a good fit for this adaptation of culture and process because microservices, due to their characteristics, closely support DevOps processes.

2. **Speed up existing applications using fast monoliths**: *"Accelerate existing applications by migrating to a modern, container-based platform – and break up monolithic applications into microservices or miniservices for additional efficiency gains."* Eclipse MicroProfile can be of great help when breaking up your monolith into microservices. As you identify bounded contexts in your monolith, consider using Eclipse MicroProfile to implement each of the microservices that implement the logic of each bounded context.

3. **Use application services to speed up development**: *"Speed up software development with reusability. Cloud-native application services are ready-to-use developer tools. However, these reusable components must be optimized and integrated into the underlying cloud-native infrastructure to maximize their benefits."* An **In-Memory Data Grid** (**IMDG**) and Messaging Brokers are application services that help speed up the development of business logic. A microservice, developed using Eclipse MicroProfile, can leverage these application services by invoking them from within its method bodies. Eclipse MicroProfile does not impose any kind of restriction when integrating to application services, such as an IMDG or a Messaging Broker.

4. **Choose the right tool for the right task**: *"Use a container-based application platform that supports the right mix of frameworks, languages, and architectures – and can be tailored to your specific business application need."* Eclipse MicroProfile is one of the tools that a developer can use when choosing the right tool for the right task. For example, Red Hat Application Runtimes is a collection of runtimes and tools, which includes Eclipse MicroProfile, Node.js, Spring Boot, and Vertex.

5. **Provide developers with a self-service, on-demand infrastructure**: *"Use containers and container orchestration technologies to simplify access to the underlying infrastructure, give control and visibility to IT operations teams, and provide robust application life cycle management across various infrastructure environments, such as data centers, private clouds, and public clouds."* The microservices you develop with Eclipse MicroProfile can be deployed to one or more containers. By easily managing these containers and your microservices architecture, which is running on them, you can accelerate your development cycles to deliver value to the business faster.

6. **Automate IT to accelerate application delivery**: "*Create automation sandboxes in order to learn about the automation language and process, establish collaborative dialog across organizations for defining service requirements, create self-service catalogs that empower users and speed delivery, and use metering, monitoring, and chargeback policies and processes.*" Eclipse MicroProfile provides capabilities for metrics, fault tolerance, and health checks, all of which can be used as input to the IT automation processes.

7. **Implement continuous delivery and advanced deployment techniques**: "*Accelerate the delivery of your cloud-native applications with automated delivery, CI/CD pipelines, rolling blue/green and canary deployments, and A/B testing.*" The use of microservices in combination with CI/CD can facilitate advanced deployment techniques. For example, you can introduce a MicroProfile-based microservice with new functionality as part of a blue/green or canary deployment into production and switch all of the traffic to it once you have proven that the new functionality works as expected.

8. **Evolve a more modular architecture**: "*Choose a modular design that makes sense for your specific needs, using microservices, a monolith-first approach, or miniservices – or a combination.*" For this step, you can use Eclipse MicroProfile to develop microservices for new applications or as you break specific bounded contexts of your monolith into microservices.

Now that we have discussed how Eclipse MicroProfile facilitates cloud-native application development and how it can help in each of the eight steps to guide you in your journey to cloud-native applications, let's turn to the topic of running MicroProfile-based applications across clouds.

# Developing and running MicroProfile applications across clouds

What features does MicroProfile provide to support development across clouds? Microservices and support for language-agnostic communication based on HTTP REST API are two of the main features that are supported. In addition, MicroProfile Config supports the integration of cloud environment variables that define integration with the cloud environment. MicroProfile Health Check supports integration with the cloud environment health checks. MicroProfile Metrics and MicroProfile OpenTracing support integration with the DevOps monitoring tasks. Finally, MicroProfile fault tolerance supports fallback and recovery behaviors between the independent microservices.

Eclipse MicroProfile provides capabilities that allow for the development of microservices and applications across clouds. But what about the underlying cloud compute resources that are being used? Does it matter if a MicroProfile-based application is running on bare-metal machines, VMs, or containers? We will discuss that now.

# Bare-metal machines versus VMs versus containers

The decision of whether to run a MicroProfile-based microservice or application on bare-metal machines, VMs, or containers depends on the specific requirements of your application. In fact, the determination of what type of underlying cloud compute resource rests squarely on your application needs and not the framework being used for its development, that is, Eclipse MicroProfile. For example, if your application or microservice requires real or near-real-time response times, then you'd most likely favor a bare-metal or container (running on bare-metal) deployment. This decision would be made independent of the framework you are using to write your business logic, whether that be Eclipse MicroProfile or another one.

Since Eclipse MicroProfile supports microservices and language-agnostic communication based on HTTP REST, your inter-microservice communication is unaffected by the type of underlying compute on which your microservices are running; for example, you could have a microservice running on a VM communicating via REST with another microservice running on a bare-metal machine. But what if your application consists of microservices running on-premises and another running on the cloud, also known as a hybrid cloud application? What considerations do you need to have in mind?

# Considerations when using MicroProfile in a hybrid cloud deployment

A hybrid cloud application comprises on-premises logic as well as on-cloud logic. In other words, if part of your application logic runs on-premises and part of it runs in the cloud, you effectively have a hybrid cloud application. When using Eclipse MicroProfile in this type of deployment, here are the things you need to consider:

- Configuration of communication routes between the cloud environment and the on-premises environment needs to be done using whatever DNS support the cloud environment supports

- Configuration of MicroProfile OpenTracing to enable the capture of tracing across cloud environments
- Monitoring of the split MicroProfile Metrics information across cloud environments
- Setting up CI tasks to target the appropriate cloud environment in order to maintain the correct microservices

Out of the preceding list, MicroProfile OpenTracing presents challenges that are unique. These will be discussed in the following section.

# Challenges when using MicroProfile OpenTracing in a multi-cloud deployment

Distributed tracing in a multi-cloud environment can be challenging. We want to fulfill the same objective that we would with a single cloud environment, that is, to visualize the single end-to-end trace associated with a request as it passes through services within and across each cloud, but may face complications when dealing with different context propagation formats and storage of the tracing data in different formats per cloud.

The first challenge is to ensure that a trace continues across different cloud environments. This is a problem because, at the time of writing this book, there is not a widely adopted or standardized trace context format. Usually, each tracing system uses different headers and formats to propagate the tracing context. For instance, Zipkin uses B3 propagation, Jaeger uses a `ber-trace-id` header, Amazon X-Ray uses `X-Amzn-Trace-Id`, and Google uses `X-Cloud-Trace-Context`. Therefore, if a request has to be traced across heterogenous tracing systems, each time it leaves or enters a different environment, the trace context has to be converted. This can usually be done by configuring a tracer with a custom injector or extractor implementation. However, this is currently beyond the scope of the MicroProfile OpenTracing project. In the future, the trace context format might be standardized under the W3C Trace Context project (`https://www.w3.org/TR/trace-context/`).

The second challenge, even in a homogenous tracing environment, is to visualize tracing data from multi-cloud environments. This can be problematic because tracing data in each cloud might be stored in different databases or in different formats. This can be overcome by replicating the data to a single unified storage or sending missing tracing data between systems on-demand with the appropriate data format adjustments.

Next, we will discuss the challenges of using Eclipse MicroProfile in a service mesh, such as Istio.

# Considerations when using Eclipse MicroProfile in a service mesh

Service meshes such as Istio or LinkerD offer services at the platform level on top of Kubernetes in the areas of discovery, routing, and fault tolerance. Some of those services can also be found in MicroProfile. When you deploy a MicroProfile application into such a service mesh, you need to consider whether you want to use the version from MicroProfile or the one from the mesh.

The MicroProfile feature that is most likely affected here is fault tolerance, especially the retry logic.

## Retry

Retry in fault tolerance lets you retry a request to another service in case the first request fails (see Chapter 3, *MicroProfile Config and Fault Tolerance*, for more information). Now, consider that you have the following code:

```
@Retry (maxRetries = 3)
void aMethod() {
    callBackend();
}
```

Although this tells Istio to retry 5 times, you may end up with 15 retries (Istio will retry 5 times for each of the 3 retries in your code before it returns an error) before aMethod finally ends with an error. You may consider turning off the retries in code, as changes to the number of retries in Istio can be made on the fly without the need to restart a pod.

## Fallback

On the other hand, Istio does not have a fallback policy for when all the retries fail – it is not possible to have Istio call another version of your workload. When you annotate the preceding code with the @Fallback annotation, it is possible to execute another action in case the original call fails:

```
@Fallback(fallbackMethod = "fallbackForA")
@Retry (maxRetries = 3)
string aMethod() {
    callBackend();
}
```

```
void String fallbackForA() {
    return "A cached string";
}
```

In this case, the `fallbackForA` fallback method will be called once all the retries from Istio, times those from MicroProfile, have been exhausted. If you remove the `@Retry` annotation from the preceding example, the fallback method is called when the Istio retries have been exhausted.

# Fault injection in the service mesh

Istio lets you inject faults into the results pretty easily. This sounds counterproductive at the start, but can be a very nice way of testing that you get the fault tolerance handling right. The following `VirtualService` for Istio defines such fault injection:

```
apiVersion: networking.istio.io/v1alpha3
kind: VirtualService
metadata:
  name: fault-injection-service
spec:
  hosts:
  - myTarget
  http:
  - route:
    - destination:
      host: myTarget
    fault:
      abort:
        httpStatus: 404
        percent: 20
      delay:
        percent: 50
        fixedDelay: 200ms
```

Istio will hear for calls to the destination host, `myTarget`, and send a 404 response for 20% of the calls instead of the real response code. On top of this, it will delay every other response by 200 milliseconds.

# Conclusion

MicroProfile defines primitives in the area of fault tolerance that can also be provided by other means, such as in a service mesh. If this is the case for you, you have to consider which one to activate. Activating both may result in unexpected behavior.

# Summary

In this chapter, you have learned how Eclipse MicroProfile facilitates cloud-native application development, regardless of whether it is a hybrid cloud or multi-cloud application. We also discussed the relationship between microservices, cloud-native development, and container-native development, and how microservices running on containers are an ideal option for cloud-native development. You also learned how Eclipse MicroProfile relates to the 12-factor app, as well as serverless and FaaS environments.

We covered the eight steps to guide your journey into cloud-native applications and how Eclipse MicroProfile can help at each step. In addition, we discussed what you need to consider when using Eclipse MicroProfile for applications that span across clouds, when to run Eclipse MicroProfile on bare-metal machines versus VMs versus containers, what to consider when running Eclipse MicroProfile microservices in hybrid cloud applications, the challenges to be aware of when running Eclipse MicroProfile OpenTracing in a multi-cloud deployment, and finally what to consider when using Eclipse MicroProfile in a service mesh.

Throughout this book, we've covered the origins of MicroProfile, a specification for Java microservices, and the history behind how it came into being. We introduced the open source project, its mission, governance, benefits, how to contribute to it, and the life cycle of its sub-projects. We then delved into each of the MicroProfile APIs/sub-projects that make up the umbrella/platform release, as well as the sub-projects outside the umbrella release.

We also covered the current implementations of MicroProfile in the market, including Quarkus, and showed you how to "quark" a generated MicroProfile project by the MicroProfile Starter. We discussed the Conference Application, a community sample project that demonstrates the interoperability of MicroProfile across different vendor implementations. We also provided code examples throughout for reference and discussion purposes, and also provided a fully working project with source code that implemented all the MicroProfile APIs that you can freely access, download, compile, and reuse in your development efforts and to get jump-started with MicroProfile. Later, we discussed the reactive functionality offered by MicroProfile and its future developments, such as sub-projects in the pipeline and in the MicroProfile sandbox, as well as its likely future relationship with Jakarta EE.

Lastly, we went over how MicroProfile-based applications and microservices are a good fit for implementing solutions in containers, the cloud, and serverless/FaaS deployments. Whether you are new to Java microservices or an experienced Java developer, you can use all the knowledge you have gained from this book to start developing microservices that are based on this new and innovative community-driven specification for the creation of observable, scalable, secure, and highly available hybrid and multi-cloud applications so that you can deliver value to your business faster.

# Questions

1. How does Eclipse MicroProfile facilitate cloud-native application development?
2. What are the two complementary concerns of cloud-native application development? How does Eclipse MicroProfile fit into these concerns?
3. What are the four key tenets of cloud-native application development? How does Eclipse MicroProfile relate to these?
4. How does Eclipse MicroProfile contribute to each of the eight steps to guide your journey through cloud-native applications?
5. How does Eclipse MicroProfile relate to the 12-factor app?
6. How can Eclipse MicroProfile facilitate serverless and FaaS environments?
7. What should you consider when implementing and running Eclipse MicroProfile across clouds?
8. What are the challenges when using Eclipse MicroProfile OpenTracing in a multi-cloud deployment?
9. What should you consider when using Eclipse MicroProfile in a service mesh?

# Assessments

## Chapter 1

1. An enterprise Java microservice has the following features:

    - It is written using the Java language.
    - It can use any Java framework.
    - It can use any Java APIs.
    - It must be enterprise-grade: reliable, available, scalable, secure, robust, and performant.
    - It must fulfill the characteristics of microservice architectures as listed at `https://martinfowler.com/microservices/`, which are as follows:
        - Componentization via services
        - Organized around business capabilities
        - Products not projects
        - Smart endpoints and dumb pipes
        - Decentralized governance
        - Decentralized data management
        - Infrastructure automation
        - Design for failure
        - Evolutionary design

2. The terms digital economy and digital transformation describe the convergence of four different forces that are changing the needs of businesses: mobile, cloud, IoT, and open source.

3. Businesses need to adapt to the new demands of the digital economy. Not only do they have to create, run, and support traditional-style applications, but also such applications that need to conform to the new demands of the digital economy. They have to support both waterfall and DevOps processes, hybrid cloud infrastructures, and SOA and microservice architectures.

4. At the time of writing, and according to the TIOBI index and others, Java is the #1 or #2 most popular language for programming at organizations. With an estimated more than 10 million Java programmers worldwide, Java is still very relevant and important to companies, vendors, and the community at large, who are all heavily invested in Java and are hungry to continue to leverage the expertise and experience of their Java developers.

5. The slowdown in innovation in the Java EE specification was one of the key reasons that caused MicroProfile to come into existence.

6. At the time of writing this book, Eclipse MicroProfile consists of 12 APIs (or sub-projects) under the project umbrella. Four of them come from Java EE APIs (CDI, JSON-P, JAX-RS, and JSON-B), and the remaining eight are created by the MicroProfile project. The 12 APIs are as follows:
    - Config
    - Fault Tolerance
    - JWT Propagation
    - Health Check
    - Metrics
    - Open API
    - Open Tracing
    - REST Client
    - CDI (a specification from Java EE)
    - JSON-P (a specification from Java EE)
    - JAX-RS (a specification from Java EE)
    - JSON-B (a specification from Java EE)

7. Health Check and Metrics in Eclipse MicroProfile 3.0 introduced the first breaking changes.

8. In addition to the general benefits of microservices, Eclipse MicroProfile particularly provides:

    - The benefits of community collaboration: Eclipse MicroProfile is an open source project run by the community. No single vendor controls or determines the evolution and maturation of the specification.
    - Freedom of choice of implementation: Many vendors have implemented Eclipse MicroProfile as part of their software stacks and customers have the option to select whichever implementation is the most appropriate for their environment.

- Faster evolution: Since Eclipse MicroProfile is an innovation project, new and improved functionality is delivered frequently in time-boxed releases. This allows developers and customers to have these at their fingertips and start leveraging updates in their projects sooner rather than later.
- Based on decades of experience: Not only do the specifications subject-matter experts bring with them a vast wealth of experience, expertise, and knowledge, but Eclipse MicroProfile also leverages market-tested and production-proven capabilities in the Java EE APIs that it builds upon, offering maturity to developers.
- Familiarity with enterprise Java: Eclipse MicroProfile builds upon familiar enterprise Java constructs, making it easy for enterprise Java developers to adopt.
- No re-training needed: Your existing enterprise Java developers will find Eclipse MicroProfile to be a natural progression of their expertise. There is little to no learning curve. They will be able to leverage their skills.
- Interoperability: The different MicroProfile implementations are interoperable with each other, providing users the freedom to select one or combine many MicroProfile implementations in an application.
- Multiple ways to use the APIs: Eclipse MicroProfile APIs provide easy-to-use interfaces, such as CDI-based, programmatic, command-line, and file-based (configuration-based).
- Thorough set of artifacts: Each API includes a Test Compatibility Kit (TCK), Javadoc, PDF document for download, API Maven artifact coordinates, Git tags, and downloads (specification and source code).

# Chapter 2

1. The main means of communication for the MicroProfile community is their Google Group, called *Eclipse MicroProfile*. You can post a message to it by sending an email to `microprofile@googlegroups.com`. Another great way to get your voice heard is by attending the bi-weekly MicroProfile Hangout call. Please check the MicroProfile Google Calendar to find out the exact date, time, and meeting information to join.

2. The MicroProfile Hangout call serves as a forum where topics brought up by attendees are discussed and decisions are made, from sub-project statuses and release contents to release dates and sub-project creation approvals.

3. A sub-project (MicroProfile specification) lead or a group of leads are usually subject-matter experts in the topic at hand and are designated to serve as its facilitators. One important aspect to note is that the lead or leads of a working group (or sub-project for that matter) do not single-handedly shape or determine the evolution of a specification or what capabilities are included or not. They do not have veto power or a final say in the decisions made with respect to their specification. By sharing of ideas, expertise, past experiences, analysis of existing technologies, and best practices, the working group will come up with their best proposal possible.

4. After the community discusses a new idea at length in the MicroProfile Google Group and/or the MicroProfile Hangout call, and it's been determined that it is worth furthering the debate, the community decides to create a working group for this new idea, and a lead or a group of leads, who are usually subject-matter experts in the topic at hand, are designated to serve as its facilitators. The working group will establish a recurring weekly or bi-weekly meeting, which is entered in the MicroProfile Google Calendar. Anybody can attend these meetings, but there's usually a core number of people that serve as the subject-matter experts that participate in these calls. After a few meetings, the working group decides whether or not the new functionality should be brought up to the MicroProfile Hangout call to discuss its proposal to become a MicroProfile sub-project. At the MicroProfile Hangout call, a sub-project proposal may be rejected or accepted. The acceptance of a sub-project means that it effectively addresses a need that enriches the specification towards its goal of optimizing enterprise Java for a microservices architecture. It is at this moment, that a sub-project becomes an official MicroProfile API. Once the sub-project becomes a MicroProfile API, then a determination is made whether it should be a standalone sub-project outside the umbrella or a sub-project included in the umbrella of MicroProfile releases.

5. Eclipse MicroProfile follows a time-boxed rapid incremental release schedule, which is public and listed on the Eclipse Foundation MicroProfile Project page. Major Eclipse MicroProfile releases, for example, from 1.x to 2.x, include major updates to MicroProfile APIs that may introduce breaking changes. Minor releases, that is, point releases, include small API updates or new APIs that make the predetermined release date. Currently, the MicroProfile community release windows are in February, June, and November of every year for minor and/or major releases.

6. The sandbox repository, which is a GitHub repository, is for incubating ideas and code examples that will eventually turn into a separate repository, contributing to a new specification. Anybody can open pull requests and use the sandbox for experimentation of new ideas and to share code and documentation, which can be used as part of the discussion in the community Google Group, the MicroProfile Hangout calls, or working group meetings.

7. The reason for releasing a sub-project outside the MicroProfile umbrella/platform release is that it gives the community and end users an opportunity to utilize and test the new technology, hence proving it in real applications before it can be considered for inclusion to the umbrella. The MicroProfile project encourages that a new sub-project specification at least release one version outside the umbrella before its inclusion in the umbrella/platform release can be considered.

8. The MicroProfile Starter is a samples source code generator, whose goal is to aid developers to quickly get started using and exploiting the capabilities of the community-driven open source specification for enterprise Java microservices, Eclipse MicroProfile, by generating working sample code in a Maven project.

# Chapter 3

1. The default sources of configuration properties are environment variables, Java system properties, and the `META-INF/microprofile-config.properties` file.

2. You can provide a custom ConfigSource implementation that maps property names to values in the custom source.

3. Strings are not the only supported types, as MP-Config supports type conversion via a pluggable SPI, and provides several default conversions by default.

4. You do not need to provide a value for an injected property if you have given a `defaultValue`, or have injected the property as an `Optional<?>` value.

5. Complex property types can be handled using a custom `Converter<?>` implementation that takes a string and returns the complex type.

6. When an annotation is specified at the class level, it applies to all methods of the class.

7. False: there are currently six MP-FT policies.

8. No: we can configure `@Retry` to only retry for certain exception types.

9. No: most MP-FT annotation settings can be overridden with MP-Config properties that the MP-FT specification defines.

# Chapter 4

1. The wire format is not usable in environments that only look at the HTTP status code to determine the HC status.
2. An MP-HC response can include arbitrary properties using the `HealthCheckResponse#withData()` methods.
3. You can create a HealthCheck implementation for each service, and the MP-HC feature will logically combine them to produce an overall status response.
4. A JWT is a JSON Web Token, a JSON-formatted object that has a header, payload, and signature component.
5. A claim is a single named value from the JWT payload.
6. Anything that can be represented in JSON can be used in a JWT.
7. The single main step in authenticating a JWT is validating that it is signed via the RS256 algorithm based on a configured public key.
8. One could look at claims other that the groups claim to make checks to add application specific authorization decisions.

# Chapter 5

1. Distributed tracing provides a micro-view of what happened with a request from end to end, whereas metrics expose scalar numerical values from a single component.
2. Distributed tracing systems usually provide features such as the root cause and critical path analysis, contextualized logging, distributed context propagation, and service dependency diagrams.
3. Automatically traced are JAX-RS server endpoints and MicroProfile Rest clients. Some vendors can also automatically trace JAX-RS clients.
4. These tags are added for every REST request `http.method`, `http.status_code`, `http.url`, `component`, `span.kind` and `error` if an exception is thrown.
5. Explicit instrumentation can be added by using `@Traced` annotation or injecting the tracer and creating spans manually.
6. There are three scopes: `base` for server metrics that apply to all runtimes, `vendor` for metrics that are server-specific, and `application` for application metrics. The latter can be supplied in the user's application.

7. The output format is determined by REST content negotiation: if the `Accepts` Header is set to `application/json`, the JSON form is emitted. If the header is either `text/plain` or omitted, then the OpenMetrics format is returned.
8. Application metrics can either be supplied via annotations (`@Counted`) or programmatically.

# Chapter 6

1. No: by default, any REST endpoint will have OpenAPI generated for it even if none of the MP OpenAPI annotations are used.
2. Yes: you can choose to use as many or as few of the MP OpenAPI annotations as you wish, to represent the REST endpoints in your microservice.
3. The notion is that you predefine the expected contracts of your endpoints and encapsulate these in OpenAPI documents that can be bundled with your microservice.
4. No: you just need to know what the formats of the request and response are, and then you can create your own type-safe interface.
5. By using the `.../mp-rest/url` MP Config setting, where `...` is either the interface name of the type-safe interface or the configKey passed to the `RegisterRestClient` annotation.
6. One way is to register a `ClientHeadersFactory` implementation. Another is to list the headers in the `org.eclipse.microprofile.rest.client.propagateHeaders` MP-Config property.

# Chapter 7

1. At the time of writing, there are eight implementations of Eclipse MicroProfile, all of which are open source. They are Thorntail, Open Liberty, Apache TomEE, Payara Micro, Hammock, KumuluzEE, Launcher, and Helidon. There is also Quarkus as the latest entrant.

2. An application server is a container for Java EE applications. An application assembler only includes the functionality that the application needs, instead of requiring an application server to be up and running, and commonly generates an executable JAR. An application assembler can generate an uberjar, a self-contained runnable JAR file, or an application jar with its runtime dependencies located in a sub-directory, for example, an accompanying `lib` or `libs` sub-directory.

3. Here is a short description of the current eight MicroProfile implementations on the market:

   1. Red Hat are the sponsors of the open source Thorntail project, which implements the Eclipse MicroProfile specification. Thorntail is an application assembler that packages just the server runtime components required by your application, and creates a runnable JAR.

   2. IBM are the sponsors of the open source Open Liberty project, which implements the Eclipse MicroProfile specification. Open Liberty is the upstream open source project for the IBM WebSphere Liberty application server. Open Liberty is an application server capable of generating an uberjar, which contains your application with an embedded Open Liberty server inside it.

   3. Tomitribe are the sponsors of the open source TomEE project, which implements the Eclipse MicroProfile specification. Apache TomEE is assembled from Apache Tomcat with added Java EE features. TomEE is Java EE 6 Web Profile certified. As its GitHub describes it, "*Apache TomEE is a lightweight, yet powerful, JavaEE Application server with feature rich tooling.*"

   4. Payara are the sponsors of the open source Payara Micro project, which implements the Eclipse MicroProfile specification. Payara Server is based on the open source GlassFish application server. Payara Micro is based on Payara Server, albeit a slimmed down version of it. As their website describes, "*Payara Micro is the microservices-ready version of Payara Server.*"

   5. Hammock is an opinionated Microservices framework for building applications. It is a CDI-based framework, meaning that it is on a CDI container with CDI-based beans that run in it. John Ament is the sponsor of the open source Hammock project, which implements the Eclipse MicroProfile specification. Similar to Thorntail, Hammock is an application assembler that generates uberjars.

6. Sunesis are the sponsors of the open source KumuluzEE project, which implements the Eclipse MicroProfile specification. KumuluzEE defines itself as a lightweight microservices framework using Java and Java EE technologies and as an Eclipse MicroProfile compliant implementation. KumuluzEE allows you to bootstrap a Java EE application using just the components that you need, and it also supports the packing and running microservices as uberjars.

7. Fujitsu are the sponsors of the open source Launcher project, which implements the Eclipse MicroProfile specification. Launcher leverages an embedded GlassFish server and Apache Geronimo MicroProfile API implementations.

8. Oracle Corporation are the sponsors of the open source Helidon project, which implements the Eclipse MicroProfile specification. Helidon is a set of Java libraries that enable a developer to write microservices. It leverages Netty, a non-blocking I/O client server framework. Helidon is an application assembler in that it generates application jars.

4. Quarkus is a Kubernetes-native Java stack with the capability of compiling to native machine language or building to HotSpot (OpenJDK). When using Quarkus, your application consumes very little memory, has great performance that allows it to handle a high throughput of invocations, and has a very fast startup time (boot plus first response time), making Quarkus a great runtime for containers, cloud-native, and serverless deployments. Quarkus also provides an extension framework that allows the "quarking" of libraries and projects to make them seamlessly work under Quarkus.

5. Compile-time boot is the process that Quarkus applies to a Java application at build time to resolve all the dynamic aspects of the language that usually happen at runtime. For example, classpath scanning, reflection, configuration parsing, gathering metadata, and building runtime model are steps that Quarkus performs at build time.

6. Containers, cloud, serverless, and Function-as-a-Service deployments.

7. Quarkus provides an extension framework that allows the *quarking* of libraries and projects to make them seamlessly work under Quarkus.

8. The Conference Application showcases the integration and interoperability of different MicroProfile vendor implementations.

# Chapter 8

1. We have seen many examples throughout the book and this chapter that MP-Config settings affect both application and MP features.
2. As long as the path you supplied exists, you should be able to see a successful heath check with information about that path.
3. It shows information about the KeyCloak server. If KeyCloak is stopped, it shows an error.
4. It will not be found because the metric is generated lazily on first request.
5. TBD.
6. For unsecured methods the behavior should be similar. For secured methods, the Swagger-UI invocations fail.
7. You will see error responses.
8. That is the encoded MP-JWT. You can use that in a curl command as the *Authorization: Bearer ...* header value where you would replace the ... with the string found in the Access Base64 Token field.

# Chapter 9

1. MicroProfile Reactive Messaging is a great option for handling message sources via connectors, especially in situations where the source is generating messages at a high frequency and an asynchronous approach to processing them makes the most sense.
2. MicroProfile Context Propagation best supports MicroProfile Reactive Streams Operators and MicroProfile Reactive Messaging in that it allows the propagation of context that was traditionally associated with the current thread across various types of units of work.
3. The current specifications that support reactive programming are MicroProfile Reactive Streams Operators, MicroProfile Reactive Messaging, and MicroProfile Context Propagation.
4. At the time of writing, the projects that sit outside the Eclipse MicroProfile umbrella release are as follows:
   - Reactive Streams Operators
   - Reactive Messaging
   - Long Running Actions
   - Context Propagation
   - GraphQL

5. The MicroProfile Project sandbox is a place where the community can ideate by trying out an implementation of features and capabilities to elicit feedback, discussion, and evaluation from the community with the goal of deciding whether or not the idea should become a new API/specification for the MicroProfile project.

6. At the time of writing, the MicroProfile Boost is under community evaluation in the MicroProfile sandbox.

7. At the time of writing, Eclipse MicroProfile and Jakarta EE are two separate projects.

8. Although MicroProfile leverages four APIs from Java EE (and will most likely update these to their Jakarta EE equivalents when Jakarta EE is released), it does have thirteen APIs of its own. MicroProfile has an aggressive release cadence and is an engine of constant innovation that does not promise backward compatibility, whereas Jakarta EE has a slower release cadence with a backward compatibility promise. There are other differences between these two projects that warrant their continued autonomous development. However, their relationship is to be determined in the future.

# Chapter 10

1. Eclipse MicroProfile provide one of the best approaches to develop microservices using enterprise Java. In turn, microservices developed using containers as their unit of deployment provide one of the best approaches to develop highly distributed systems in the cloud and on-premises, that is, cloud-native applications. Hence, MicroProfile-based microservices facilitate the development of cloud-native applications.

2. There are two complementary aspects or components to cloud-native application development: application services and infrastructure services. Application services speed up the development of business logic of a cloud-native application, and infrastructure services speed up its delivery and deployment. These two aspects are complementary and integral to cloud-native application development.

3. Cloud-native application development is an approach to building and running applications that takes full advantage of the cloud computing model based upon four key tenets: a) A service-based architecture (miniservices, microservices, SOA services, and so on); b) An API-driven approach for inter-service communication; c) An underlying infrastructure that's based on containers; and d) DevOps processes. The architecture and communication aspects are related to the development concerns of cloud-native applications, and the infrastructure and the process aspects are related to their delivery/deployment. Eclipse MicroProfile relates to these tenets in that it supports the implementation of microservices that can be part of an architecture that uses containers as its underlying infrastructure, where microservices communicate with each other using their APIs, and are developed using DevOps processes.

4. This is how Eclipse MicroProfile contributes to each of the eight steps to guide your journey to cloud-native applications:

    1. Evolve a DevOps culture and practices: "Take advantage of new technology, faster approaches, and tighter collaboration by embracing the principles and cultural values of DevOps and organizing your organization around those values." Although this is an organizational and process-related step, Eclipse MicroProfile, as a specification for microservices, can be a good fit for this adaptation of culture and process because microservices, due to its characteristics, closely support DevOps processes.

    2. Speed up existing applications using fast monoliths: "Accelerate existing applications by migrating to a modern, container-based platform—and break up monolithic applications into microservices or miniservices for additional efficiency gains." Eclipse MicroProfile can be of great help when breaking up your monolith into microservices. As you identify bounded contexts in your monolith, consider using Eclipse MicroProfile to implement each of the microservices that implement the logic of each bounded context.

3. Use application services to speed up development: "Speed software development with reusability. Cloud-native application services are ready-to-use developer tools. However, these reusable components must be optimized and integrated into the underlying cloud-native infrastructure to maximize benefits." An In-Memory-Data-Grid (IMDG) and a messaging broker are application services that help speed up the development of business logic. A microservice, developed using Eclipse MicroProfile, can leverage these application services by invoking them from within its method bodies. Eclipse MicroProfile does not impose any kind of restriction when integrating to application services, such as an IMDG or a messaging broker.

4. Choose the right tool for the right task: "Use a container-based application platform that supports the right mix of frameworks, languages, and architectures—and can be tailored to your specific business application need." Eclipse MicroProfile is one of these tools that a developer can use when choosing the right tool for the right task. For example, Red Hat Application Runtimes is a collection of runtimes and tools, which includes Eclipse MicroProfile, Node.js, Spring Boot, and Vert.x.

5. Provide developers with self-service on-demand infrastructure: "Use containers and container orchestration technology to simplify access to underlying infrastructure, give control and visibility to IT operations teams, and provide robust application life-cycle management across various infrastructure environments, such as datacenters, private clouds, and public clouds." The microservices you develop with Eclipse MicroProfile can be deployed to one or more containers. By easily managing these containers and your microservices architecture running on them, you can accelerate your development cycles to deliver value to the business faster.

6. Automate IT to accelerate application delivery: "Create automation sandboxes for learning the automation language and process, establish collaborative dialog across organizations for defining service requirements, create self-service catalogs that empower users and speed delivery, and use metering, monitoring, and chargeback policies and processes." Eclipse MicroProfile provides capabilities for metrics, fault tolerance, and health checks, all of which can be used as input to the IT automation processes.

7. Implement continuous delivery and advanced deployment techniques: "Accelerate the delivery of your cloud-native applications with automated delivery, continuous integration/continuous delivery (CI/CD) pipelines, rolling blue/green and canary deployments, and A/B testing." The use of microservices in combination with CI/CD can facilitate advanced deployment techniques. For example, you can introduce a MicroProfile-based microservice with new functionality as part of a blue/green or canary deployment intro production, and switch all of the traffic to it once you have proven that the new functionality works as expected.

8. Evolve a more modular architecture: "Choose a modular design that makes sense for your specific needs, using microservices, a monolith-first approach, or miniservices—or a combination." For this step, you can use Eclipse MicroProfile to develop microservices for new applications or as you break specific bounded contexts of your monolith into microservices.

5. Twelve-factor app is a methodology that a developer can follow while designing and implementing microservices and applications, independent of the programming language or framework being used to implement them. The framework that a developer can use to implement microservices using twelve-factor app is Eclipse MicroProfile. Twelve-factor app and Eclipse MicroProfile are not mutually exclusive, but are complementary to each other.

6. Most, if not all, market FaaS offerings support Java. As such, developers can write the function bodies in one of the many implementations of Eclipse MicroProfile, which are all in Java. The ease of use and rich functionality of Eclipse MicroProfile combined with the simplicity of a FaaS platform can greatly improve the ability of developers to deliver value to the business faster. In addition, a technology such as Quarkus, which implements Eclipse MicroProfile, uses low amounts of memory and has fast startup times, is an ideal runtime for a FaaS.

7. When using Eclipse MicroProfile in a deployment across clouds, here are the things you need to consider:

   - Configuration of communication routes between the cloud environment and the on-premise environment needs to be done using whatever DNS support the cloud environment provides.
   - Configuration of MicroProfile OpenTracing to enable capture of tracing across the cloud environments.

- Monitoring of the split MicroProfile Metrics information across the cloud environments
- Setting up the CI tasks to target the appropriate cloud environment to maintain the correct microservices.

8. Distributed tracing in a multi-cloud environment can be challenging. We want to fulfill the same objective as with a single cloud environment to visualize the single end-to-end trace associated with a request as it passes through services within and across each cloud, but may face complications when dealing with different context propagation formats and storage of the tracing data in different formats per cloud. The first challenge is to ensure that a trace continues across different cloud environments. This is a problem because, at the time of writing, there is not widely adopted or standardized trace context format. Usually, each tracing system uses different headers and formats to propagate the tracing context. The second challenge, even in a homogenous tracing environment, is to visualize tracing data from multi-cloud environments. This can be problematic because tracing data in each cloud might be stored in different databases or in different formats. This can be overcome by replicating the data to a single unified storage or sending missing tracing data between systems on-demand with the appropriate data format adjustments.

9. Service Meshes such as Istio or LinkerD offer services at the platform level on top of Kubernetes in the areas of discovery, routing, and fault tolerance. Some of those services can also be found in MicroProfile. When you deploy a MicroProfile application into such a Service Mesh, you need to consider if you want to use the version from MicroProfile or the one from the Mesh. The MicroProfile feature that is most likely affected here is Fault Tolerance, and especially the retry logic.

# Other Books You May Enjoy

If you enjoyed this book, you may be interested in these other books by Packt:

**Mastering Microservices with Java - Third Edition**
Sourabh Sharma

ISBN: 978-1-78953-072-8

- Use domain-driven designs to develop and implement microservices
- Understand how to implement microservices using Spring Boot
- Explore service orchestration and distributed transactions using the Sagas
- Discover interprocess communication using **REpresentational State Transfer** (**REST**) and events
- Gain knowledge of how to implement and design reactive microservices
- Deploy and test various microservices

**Microservice Patterns and Best Practices**
Vinicius Feitosa Pacheco

ISBN: 978-1-78847-403-0

- How to break monolithic application into microservices
- Implement caching strategies, CQRS and event sourcing, and circuit breaker patterns
- Incorporate different microservice design patterns, such as shared data, aggregator, proxy, and chained
- Utilize consolidate testing patterns such as integration, signature, and monkey tests
- Secure microservices with JWT, API gateway, and single sign on
- Deploy microservices with continuous integration or delivery, Blue-Green deployment

# Leave a review - let other readers know what you think

Please share your thoughts on this book with others by leaving a review on the site that you bought it from. If you purchased the book from Amazon, please leave us an honest review on this book's Amazon page. This is vital so that other potential readers can see and use your unbiased opinion to make purchasing decisions, we can understand what our customers think about our products, and our authors can see your feedback on the title that they have worked with Packt to create. It will only take a few minutes of your time, but is valuable to other potential customers, our authors, and Packt. Thank you!

# Index

Function-as-a-Service (FaaS) 203, 207

# G

generated MicroProfile project
    making, quark 139, 140, 141, 142, 143
GraphQL
    about 198
    versus REST 198
    with databases 199

# H

Hammock
    about 133, 134
    reference link 133
Health Check Java API
    about 58, 59, 60, 62
    Health Check response messages, modifying 63
    human operators 62, 63
    integrating, with cloud platform 62
health checks
    handling, with MicroProfile 56
Helidon
    about 135
    reference link 135
hybrid cloud deployment
    consideration, when using Eclipse MicroProfile 212

# I

IANA JWT Assignments
    URL 64
In-Memory-Data-Grid (IMDG) 210
Internet of Things (IoT) 10, 12
internet scale 11

# J

Jaeger
    URL 99
    used, for MicroProfile OpenTracing 99, 100, 101
Jakarta EE 200, 201
Java Community Process (JCP) 13, 200
JSON schema syntax
    URL 57
JSON Web Token (JWT) Propagation

about 55, 64
authentication, configuring 72, 73
samples, running 73, 74, 76, 77, 79
using, in MicroProfile 64

# K

KumuluzEE
    about 134
    reference link 134

# L

Launcher
    about 135
    reference link 135
Long Running Actions (LRA) 195, 196

# M

MicroProfile 2.0
    reference link 93
MicroProfile applications
    developing, across clouds 211
    running, across clouds 211
MicroProfile Boost 199, 200
MicroProfile Config API
    @ConfigProperty annotation 40
    Config object 39, 40
    configuration, reading 38
    reference link 32
MicroProfile Config integration
    about 115
    configuration keys, simplifying 116
MicroProfile Context Propagation 189
MicroProfile Fault Tolerance API
    reference link 32
MicroProfile Health Check protocol
    about 57, 58
    recommendations 65
MicroProfile interoperability
    conference application 144, 145, 146
MicroProfile JWT (MP-JWT) Propagation 64
MicroProfile Metrics
    about 81, 82
    application-specific metrics, supplying 85, 86
    metadata 82
    retrieving, from server 83, 84

www.ingramcontent.com/pod-product-compliance
Lightning Source LLC
LaVergne TN
LVHW081521050326
832903LV00025B/1571